My Greatest Gift

Valerie Banton

I dedicate this book to our amazing children Roger, Andrew, and Ruth and our grand-children Daniel, Jessica, Chloe, Leo, Kirsty, and Oliver, who never failed to be there for me throughout the dreadful unprecedented times that Alzheimer's Disease brings, with its progression and destruction. You were always there in my times of need, and there were many times.

A moment in time as our lives unfold.
And there are many moments.
They will never be forgotten.
Neither will the love of my life, who
should not have had to suffer the awful
effects of Alzheimer's Disease

Alzheimer's Disease is a blanket of darkness, closing over the mind, slowly, slowly, then it will suddenly escalate for a time, then slow down again. It takes away the person you love. They are still there in body but not in mind. Over the years the love of my life became lost. He was no longer the wonderful loving man I married. I would have given anything at all to get him back, but Alzheimer's took him from me.

Chapter 1

The stone hit his head, below the hairline on his forehead. Wham! Bang! ………Ouch! Something was trickling down his nose over his face. He got up from his place on the edge of the large pond where he and his friend were catching fish. Brian had been practising shots with his catapult but how did he manage to hit Ian, his pal on the other side of the large fishing pond? The fish had stopped biting and Brian was bored.

They quickly packed up their gear, loaded the small cycle trailer, got on their bikes, and headed home. By now Ian's head was numb from the initial pain and the sudden shock was making him feel nauseous. He wiped the blood from his face as he rode. Not far now. Home was in sight and Ian's head was hurting. His face was deathly pale as he jumped off his bike, threw it to the ground and ran into the house in search of his mother who was confronted with her young boy covered in blood trickling from a large gash on his forehead. As an ex-nurse used to dealing with such injuries, she sprang into action and he was soon cleaned up and on the way to the hospital whilst explaining to his Mum what he thought had happened.

Years later the scar was there but his hair came down over it and it was hardly noticeable. It had faded with the passage of time. He mentioned it to the Consultant Psychiatrist who arranged for a scan to rule out any damage to his brain from the impact of the stone years ago. Thankfully, it proved negative. Ian's memory loss was apparently not due to this injury. Maybe it was simply the ageing process. Ian was 66 years old, and he was fit and healthy and life was good. Home in Spain on the Costa del Sol provided all the benefits of an idyllic lifestyle. Our little bit of paradise. Our retreat. We both loved to be there and made the most of it.

Young and in love

Chapter 2

I met Ian for the first time when we were both teenagers attending a local youth club in 1959. I was almost 15 and Ian was 17. I could not take my eyes off this handsome young man with his strikingly blonde hair. Lucky for me, Ian was smitten too, he only had eyes for me. I was a complete contrast to him with my dark brunette hair, and rosy cheeks. This was the start of a special relationship. Our love for one another blossomed and we became almost inseparable spending as much time as possible together enjoying each other's company.

In his teenage years Ian was a keen car enthusiast and had a sports car chassis on the drive at his home. He was planning to re-build the car, but time was against him. He had fitted the engine, gearbox, wheels and seats and it was driveable. He occasionally took it along the street where he lived which was an unadopted road at the time. Wanting to teach me to drive now that I was old enough to learn he took me to the local disused aerodrome across the road from his house to give me a lesson. I can remember having to hold on to the battery as Ian drove the un-finished vehicle. I thoroughly enjoyed my lesson with him. It was fun driving round the aerodrome, avoiding the potholes, perched on a chassis. He never did finish the car but instead bought an amazing 1930's Morgan 3-wheeler. We had such fun spending many hours out and about in the Morgan, in all weathers. It was open to the elements and Ian drove it everywhere he went. I remember him coming the few miles from his house to mine in the snow and when he arrived, he had frost on his eyebrows. He loved it and so did I. There were no doors to open to get in. Access into the car was over the side. Not always a very elegant way to get in avoiding the hot exhaust pipe which ran along the outside edge, especially in the short tight skirts which were fashionable at the time. Nonetheless we spent many happy exhilarating hours travelling all over Yorkshire and Derbyshire exploring the countryside. On occasions the car would stall at traffic lights which was always a nuisance. To start it again Ian had to jump out and use all his energy turning the starter handle until the engine fired up. It was always a great adventure spending time with him in the Morgan. I never did get to drive it myself but was quite happy to sit beside Ian whilst he took me out.

His lovely car was sold to help towards our bottom drawer. He got £40 for it which was a good price. We were grateful to have the money to put towards items for our home together.

We were married in February 1965.

Over the years we have occasionally tried to find out what happened to Ian's Morgan. It had never materialised, and Ian was convinced it had been scrapped. However, on researching the car myself recently in the hope that someone had kept it or was even restoring it, I was pleasantly surprised and delighted to find the car. It had sold after being restored and had fetched in the region of £38,000. I so wish I were able to tell Ian. If only we had had the foresight to keep and restore it ourselves. It certainly looks amazing.

Our sons were born in April 1967. Fraternal twins. Both breech deliveries born 4 minutes apart. Roger had dark hair and Andrew was quite fair. There was a slight difference in their weight and Andrew remained in hospital for a little while to gain some ounces. Our amazing baby boys were soon at home together and life was hectic caring for 2 small babies.

Their baby sister Ruth arrived in the August of 1970. She was born at home and her two little brothers could not stop looking at their tiny baby sister lying in her cot sucking her thumb.

Ian had worked for British Rail for a few years in the 1960's during which time he received an award for an idea he promoted to detect cracks in railway track. These cracks were quite lethal and could cause a train to de-rail. His idea was quite simply a machine pushed along the rail which released water identifying where there was a split. He received a congratulatory letter and a payment of £25 for his efforts. Eventually Ian decided to join his father's electrical business. He took over the firm on his dad's retirement and had one or two contracts with a local motor group and a firm of solicitors, retiring himself in 2004. He enjoyed his work. Most of his customers were gained by recommendation.

In 1974 we moved from our modern semi-detached property having bought a large double fronted Edwardian house in need of some renovation. This was a big change from our previous two dwellings which were both purchased as new build properties. The next few years flew by and the house took on a new persona. Ian's DIY skills were commendable and with help from us all and occasionally his Dad, an extension was built. This was one of many improvements to the house.

Building and flying model aeroplanes was a favourite pastime with twin sons, Roger, and Andrew. They would sit for hours at the dining room table, designing planes and drawing the part on tracing paper then cutting out shapes from balsa wood and sticking it all together. The plane would look remarkable with a coat of paint and numbers and emblems which helped to it to look authentic. The excitement would reach great heights as they left the house, with their completed aeroplane for its inaugural flight. Occasionally they would return with their plane in bits after crashing to the ground. There was nothing to do but start again. I always felt so upset seeing their plane in pieces knowing how many hours they had all spent building the aircraft only to see it smashed in a matter of seconds as it hit the ground.

Ian enjoyed going to The Nats, the British model flying association championships and usually built a model to take along with him. He learned a lot from watching the championships and thoroughly enjoyed himself seeing the skills of the people there who were flying the model planes.

He also had a passion for horses. He would enjoy helping Ruth with her pony and sometimes riding with her when he could borrow a horse from the farm nearby. With the help of the boys and Ruth, they built a trailer for the pony. It was immaculate. Painted in the colours, gold, black and red, to match the car used for towing. This provided many opportunities for Ruth to enter pony shows and reap the benefits of all her hard work bringing home rosettes to hang in her room.

During the 1980's we were lucky to have an opportunity of learning to Scuba Dive. This was something we had never really considered but now our children were older, we had time to do this. I had always enjoyed swimming and had been a keen swimmer having regularly attended the local pool whenever I could. However, this was not a sport Ian particularly liked. He was not a good swimmer and did think maybe he would struggle with learning to Scuba Dive. Buoyancy in the water whilst using scuba equipment is something different and he was amazed at his ability. He became a very enthusiastic diver, enjoying the open water dives as often as he could. Lessons were held at one of the local swimming pools.

We both went on to qualify as sport divers and attended several dive events around the east Yorkshire coast and the south eastern coast of Scotland. On one such occasion our team was staying in caravans off the coast of St. Abb's. After an eventful day in the water, we all went out for the evening to enjoy a meal and a drink or two. Ian and I returned to our caravan early leaving the others to finish their drinks. The next morning, we were woken around 5am by the sound of thudding noises on the roof of the caravan. Lying there listening to the pitter patter, pitter patter sounds we were also being deafened by the loud calling of seagulls telling all their mates to come and get the food they had been left. Thankfully, many seagulls arrived quickly so the food was soon gone, and all was quiet again. The rest of the team were enjoying a lie in after their efforts throwing the remains of their takeaway on our caravan roof.

Ian had been a keen cyclist in his youth taking part in team trials and local cycling events for the cycle tourist club. When he was in his late 40's he bought himself a racing bike. I was very keen to join him on the rides and we enjoyed many days and evenings out exploring the countryside and the benefits of the fresh air. We met other cyclists and became members of the cycle touring club in the area. The club would ride out every Sunday during both the Summer and Winter months riding many miles in the day, particularly in the Summer when the hours of daylight were longer. On occasions we would ride over 100 miles taking in the surrounding areas and visiting places of interest. Team members took it in turns to formulate an itinerary for the day calling at cafes for a break from being on the bikes to enjoy a bacon sandwich and a coffee or tea. A picnic was usually the order of the day for lunch sitting in relaxing areas before setting off on our return journey and maybe stopping for afternoon tea before our return home. We always thoroughly enjoyed these adventurous days out with our teammates and would feel exhilarated at the end of the day, relaxing in a nice warm bath before our evening meal. We had decided to buy a tandem and would sometimes ride out on this for a change. Ian always rode in the front and I would ensure he was kept refreshed with the occasional sweet from the back pocket of his cycle jacket, as I controlled the pedals in unison behind him. We loved it.

One Summer's day Ian was trying to tell me something. There was a wasp inside his jacket, and he could feel it crawling around. I lifted his top but could see nothing at all. Ian was sure it was in there and shouted at me to keep looking. I was so certain no wasp was lurking in there I slapped Ian all over his back. Seconds later a wasp flew out escaping from the confines of his cycle top and alarming everyone who saw it emerge. It was incredible that Ian had not been stung.

I had been lucky enough to be able to take early retirement at the age of 57. I had begun working in the NHS as a medical secretary when the children started school. Over the years other posts became available and after spending a few years as a personal secretary, I was offered the post of transport manager.

In my spare time my skills as a cake maker proved advantageous toward our income becoming a small business making and icing cakes for weddings and special occasions for family and friends. It earned a bit of extra cash and I thoroughly enjoyed doing this although it was very time consuming and hard work whilst also doing a full-time job.

Ian was always on hand to help deliver the wedding cakes and help me assemble them at the wedding venue. There was a great sense of satisfaction seeing the completed cake in all its glory and surrounded by the décor and flowers for the special day.

Chapter 3

Plans had been taking shape over the years for us to retire to a warmer climate and we spent many days and evenings researching parts of France and Spain, travelling to various areas to get a feeling for the different locations whilst viewing properties. We looked forward to enjoying the benefits of a healthier lifestyle.   I had been diagnosed with osteoarthritis, which was in the early stages and spending time in France or Spain was said to have beneficial effects for this problem. This was a plan in the making and it eventually came to fruition in 2005. The home we had lived in for over 30 years where we brought up our family whilst enjoying many eventful moments making numerous wonderful family memories, full of love and laughter, ups and downs, had eventually sold. By then our children were bringing up their own families. It was a bittersweet moment on the day we vacated our home. A home we had built together through sweat and tears and times of hardship. It was now time to move on and reap the benefits of those years.

Just a year before this Ian had begun to show signs of memory loss and I became concerned for him. I had been thinking for some time that he should see the doctor and I eventually suggested we make an appointment to discuss the problem. Ian's reply was totally unexpected and quite alarming. His immediate reaction was to ask me "are you trying to get me sectioned?" Where did that come from? Why was he suggesting that I would do this? I was horrified and somewhat hurt that Ian should think this of me. Had he realised what he was saying? Keeping calm to dispel any potential arguments I told him such a thought had never occurred to me and having a talk to the doctor may be worthwhile if there is any treatment to prevent the condition from worsening.   It took a while to persuade him that this was a sensible approach. Resulting from the discussion with the doctor Ian was advised to stop taking the medication he had been prescribed to reduce high cholesterol. He was asked to do this for six months and then to reassess the situation. There had been media reports of memory loss with patients in the USA taking statins. However, no improvement was noticed. Ian had stopped the tablets for a year, but the memory problem continued. The medication became part of the daily routine once again.

An exciting period in our lives was about to begin. The memory problem being addressed we were now able to follow our dream and begin arranging to spend time following up on previous research to assess the realities of the results. A decision was made that the costa del sol fitted the bill. It was within easy access of the UK, boasted a good climate having an average 320 days of sunshine annually and had proved from our research to have a good continuing social life in the winter months.

Chapter 4

We arranged to spend some time in southern Spain viewing properties and areas both inland and coastal, getting a taste for what appealed to us most. It was all beyond belief. A few weeks of being taken to various places by estate agents who not only showed us the fincas, villas, apartments, and town houses they had on their books, but also visited nearby beaches and places of interest in the areas around the properties. It usually involved a glass of wine or a coffee in a nearby beach bar, relaxing and taking in the local cultures and enjoying the warmth of the sun.

One stipulation Ian had made, he did not want to be where there was no greenery. A view of brown, barren land was not his ideal. Whilst abundant sunshine and warmth were all very welcome, it could be too much. He enjoyed gardening and had spent many hours in the garden at our various homes, digging, planting, re-arranging, and nurturing. Whilst southern Spain is hot during the height of summer the land becomes quite singed, but this is only for a short time. The rain comes in the winter months and maintains the greenery and colourful scenery. A very bearable climate.

Unfortunately, it was becoming difficult for Ian to help with the planning and assessing of finances which were necessary to ensure the correct decision was made. Sadly, and unbelievably, his memory problem had gradually deteriorated over time making it impossible for him to recall situations and discussions where figures were involved. He was aware we were making inroads with a view to purchasing a home in the sun but as far as costings, his memory was becoming less able to cope with such demands. I was therefore, left with the responsibility of making many of the decisions. Hopefully, the correct ones.

Following many exciting viewings and some disasters, we were nearing a decision when walking into a show apartment in Spain. Phase 4 was about to take shape and the property would be built within an anticipated period of 9 months. It had a feel-good factor, and fitted our criteria, ticking all the boxes. As it was to be a new build, we were looking forward to choosing the furniture and fittings which were to be installed for us before we moved in. We were not bringing any furniture from our home in the UK. A more modern approach was required, and we decided to purchase a furniture package. We were taken to a showroom where we spent time looking at the different packages and choosing what suited us and was within our budget. The young estate agent not only took us round the show apartment explaining our choices and costings, but we climbed back into the car with him afterwards and he took us to a beach a short distance from the apartment complex. It was an easily accessible area with many beach bars and restaurants boasting a small harbour with fancy expensive boats moored there. We all relaxed with a glass of wine, chatting about the area, and enjoying the picturesque scenery whilst looking forward to being able to return there in the future.

Within a few days of the viewing and having had time to mull it all over we visited the property agent and discussed the details in full before signing and handing over the required deposit. Just a few months to wait now until the completion date.

This was a time for celebration. Our plan was finalised. We looked forward to completion of our new home and our anticipated move to Spain. Our family back in the UK were delighted to hear the news and everyone began looking forward to the future and some enjoyable times together in the sun. The dream we had over the past few years was taking shape.

Chapter 5

Life continued happily back in the UK waiting for and planning the move to Spain. We continued to meet with friends now and again for an enjoyable meal or a coffee and family remained a big part of our lives.

Following the sale of our home we lived with Ruth and her husband Steve. He was a builder, and they had their own business and work was good. Ian's skills as an electrical contractor meant he was able to spend time assisting Steve now and again when electrical work was required. It worked well. His memory loss did not seem to impair his ability to carry out his work successfully. My time was occupied with helping in the home and I was also there if needed to look after our two grandchildren. Chloe who was then aged 8 and Leo a baby of 4 months.

Our other four grandchildren featured regularly in our lives too living not far away. Oliver and Kirsty lived about 12 miles away, and Daniel and his sister Jessica about 40 miles. They were all easily accessible and often spent time together staying over whilst their Mums and Dads had an occasional night out. Memories were being made of time spent together and we thoroughly enjoyed those times going out for bike rides, taking them swimming, to the seaside and spending holidays with them all. It was a good period in all our lives. At the time we had 2 miniature Jack Russell puppies, Pixie and Dixie and went for lots of walks with them over the years. The little dogs featured regularly in our daily routine. They had been with us since they were tiny providing many happy and hilarious moments with their antics. The boys had a paper round in their teenage years and would occasionally take the little dogs out with them stowed away in their paper bag with all the newspapers. The dogs were quite small and seemed to love hiding in the huge bags. There were many happy times over the years as our grandchildren grew. We all got on well and living not too far away made it easy to get together now and again. We would meet for long walks in nearby parks, taking our dogs around the lake, enjoying the fresh air and exercise. Or maybe book a table at a restaurant for a nice meal together. We all loved these times, and the conversation would flow. A BBQ was always a must in the summer months. Ian made a swing which he hung from the huge pear tree in the garden on the grassed area. It was always put to good use and a great source of fun for everyone. We both enjoyed our garden and tended it well.

Leaving all this behind to start a new life in Spain was something we had discussed many times, realising we would miss our family being close by having spent much of our time with them over the years. We planned to return to the UK to visit them on a regular basis and hoped they would come over to us for holidays occasionally too.

Chapter 6

A visit to view the progress of our new home was organised a few months prior to the anticipated completion. We were keen to have a look at the site to get an idea where the apartment would be and to ensure it was on course to be ready soon. We planned to have a holiday at the same time.

The first few days were spent enjoying some time on the beach across from our hotel. We had already visited this part of Spain before and stayed at the same hotel whilst looking round for somewhere suitable to buy a property. It was one of our favourite places having a large Marina within walking distance where there were many waterside restaurants and shops. It was a most pleasant experience to sit and relax with a glass of wine and a good meal watching the boats coming in and out of the harbour, as well as all the people enjoying themselves. This was the life we had been planning for many years and it was soon to become reality. We hired a car for a few days so we could visit the site where the apartment was. It was necessary to have a car as access to the area was currently unavailable by public transport although a little train ran up to the local pizzeria and it was then a short walk to the site. We had spent an hour or two in the local restaurant when viewing the show apartment and surrounding area. The views from here were quite spectacular. It was a popular restaurant with locals and tourists alike. A place where we would spend many happy hours.

It turned out to be a bit of a disappointment when we finally reached the place where phase 4 was being constructed. The whole area was surrounded by a high fence and only accessible to those working on the construction of the three apartment blocks. However, we were able to get a feel for how it might look when completed and were given an idea of where our apartment would be. We stood for a while in the afternoon sunshine trying to envisage our new home and what it would be like to live there. It was in the final phase. Most of the three phases already completed were occupied, and together with the show apartment gave us a good idea of what life would be like when we were able to move there. We were looking forward to this new venture in our lives. There were already three swimming pools and a fourth was under construction in phase 4. I was really looking forward to spending many hours in and around the pool.

2007 was a very wet Summer in the UK. The wettest on record. There was 414mm of rainfall across England and Wales from May to July – more than in any period since records began in 1766. Across Yorkshire and the Midlands, thousands of people were rescued, whole towns cut off and families forced to flee their properties.

The inclement weather in the UK was one of the reasons many residents moved abroad to better climates. The Summer of 2007 gave us even more justification for our purchase in southern Spain.

Not long after our visit to view the progress of the building works, we received exciting news! Our new home would be completed in early August. This was now becoming a reality and we would have to be extraordinarily strong leaving our family behind. That moment was drawing closer and closer. We reminded one another that this marked the start of our dream which included all the family. It had been planned for their future too. A place for us all to spend as much time as we wished to spend doing what we most enjoyed and enhancing our lives for a long time to come.

There was much to do. We began planning our move and I

sat for hours at the computer calculating the mileage from our home in the UK to the new apartment in Spain and planning a route over a period of five days, driving to Dover, and taking the ferry to Calais, enabling us to arrive at the apartment on the date of completion on 10th August 2007. The idea was to enjoy a holiday as we journeyed to our new home spending a bit of time in the areas we were passing through. We would be driving through France into Spain, a total of over 1600 miles. To drive there without stopping would take approximately 26 hours, but this was not in the plan. We would take turns to drive and average around 320 miles a day. Some days more, some days less. Things were on track and it was so exciting.

Chapter 7

The morning of Monday 6th August 2007 had arrived. Our ford focus was packed full of the items we were taking with us. None of the furniture from the home we were leaving behind would be needed for our new home. It had either been sold or passed on to family. Smaller items such as kitchen equipment and our cycles, including our tandem, sold on eBay or at a local tabletop sale. The apartment was to remain free of clutter. We were to make a completely new start. Only items of sentimental value were making the journey.

Some of the family who could be there were together at the house to say their goodbyes. We knew it would be a difficult but memorable day. Leaving our family behind would be hard! There were huge hugs all round and a few tears, but everyone remained positive looking forward to being together again quite soon for a holiday. Our grandchildren had a surprise in store. A ribbon was tied across the gate to the house. As we drove towards the ribbon it was cut by our granddaughters. A very poignant moment and a few minutes of indecision. Were we really leaving for a new life? Did we want to do this leaving behind our loving family? The reality hit us, and the tears began to flow but we had to keep going. The girls were running alongside the car, running as fast as they could to the end of the street. I really began to feel as though I could not do this and felt I wanted to go back. We could not leave these gorgeous girls. But our new life awaited us. We had no alternative, we had to go. The gorgeous girls and the rest of the wonderful loving family would be coming to see us very soon. We all waved madly at one another until disappearing out of sight. There was an overwhelming feeling of sadness tinged with excitement for what lay ahead.

The drive to Dover to take the ferry crossing to Calais was well on schedule.

We would soon be enjoying our journey spending time taking in areas of France and inland Spain on the way to our new life as we had planned.

Although I arranged the journey so that we took turns to drive it did not work out that way. Ian said he enjoyed driving and did not need a break from it. He is not a good passenger and took the wheel for most of the journey. We managed to stick to our timings and mileage each day stopping now and again for a rest and some relaxation whilst enjoying some refreshments. We had allowed time in the schedule for sightseeing and particularly enjoyed a romantic walk by the River Garonne in Bordeaux close to the hotel where we were staying overnight. It was a beautiful day and reminded us that many more days like this lay ahead.

The last night before the final leg of our journey was spent in Madrid. We still had about 350 miles to our destination. The excitement of seeing our new apartment for the first time was becoming very intense. We could not get there soon enough. It was quite hot in Madrid in August and it was good to get on the road and circulate some air inside the car. Air pollution in this area was known to be excessive and became apparent when a band of dingey orange cloud became visible in the sky hanging over the whole surrounding area. It continued for many miles. We were glad to be heading for the coast and soon left the coloured sky behind.

The excitement was mounting. We would soon be arriving at the office of the agent to collect the keys to our new home. This done we set off again along the coast road. Locating where we were going to live became a bit of a trial. Time for some guidance. It could not be far now. It was closer than we realised and only a few miles away from the agent's office. A long steep hill was negotiated through a residential area and suddenly there it was. We had arrived at our future home. A gated residential area. As soon as we entered the code to open the gate, we were on our way up to phase 4 at the top of the hill. All we had to do now was locate the correct block out of three and find the floor and apartment number. Parking our car next to the pool area we started our search.

The lift did not appear to be operating so we climbed the stairs up to our floor and looked for our door. This was so exciting.

Opening the door and walking in for the first time was surreal. This was the dream we had been building on for years. It was incredible that this moment had arrived. The apartment was fully furnished and completely ready for us. I had not expected to find the beds made, soft furnishings all in place, paintings hanging on the walls, kitchen cupboards full of crockery and pans, in fact all that was needed to get on with our new life.

Our little bit of Paradise

Chapter 8

It was extremely hot and humid. We were sitting on the patio overlooking the pool enjoying our first meal there together with a celebratory glass of wine. The dream was now a reality and we could hardly believe it after all the years of planning.

It was a Friday afternoon. In our excitement we had not thought to check that the power was on and were soon to discover the apartment had no electricity. We were determined not to let this problem spoil our enjoyment of this remarkably memorable moment. The first day in our new home. It would be dealt with. Who needs electricity? After contacting the agents to inform them of our problem we got on with our day. It was the weekend, and no-one was available to rectify the problem. They promised an electrician would be out on Monday.

A few hours later we met our new neighbours who were buying their apartment ready for their retirement in a couple of years. Pauline and Bruce were from Livingstone in west Lothian. They had electricity, but no water! After all we were in Spain and tomorrow will always do. What could we expect! We did not really need water or electricity! There was nothing else to do but look after one another and be neighbourly. It was a great introduction to new friends. The future was looking good.

Days turned into weeks and weeks into months. Our life of leisure was now in full swing. We met another couple who were moving to an apartment close by. It was nice to meet Bob and Betty who unbelievably were also from West Lothian in Scotland. We spent many hours together enjoying our new lives and exploring the area whilst becoming familiar with the cultures and language.

We occasionally flew back to the UK to catch up with

family and friends. Family would also travel to Spain to be with us when they could for a few days or weeks enjoying the sunshine and the outdoor life. It was an idyllic existence. Friends also came to stay now and again.

Throughout the weeks and months Ian's condition was being monitored. Medication to slow down the progression of his memory loss was being administered. A Consultant Psychiatrist was aware of Ian's condition and carried out routine tests from time to time to monitor any deterioration. He would ask Ian a series of routine straightforward questions such as what day it was, what city he was in, what year it was. Leo was sitting on my lap at one session when he decided to help his Grandpa with an answer. It was quite funny and made us all laugh. A record was kept of the number of correct answers Ian gave each time and thankfully he was remaining stable. We would travel back to the UK for the appointments every few months.

We never failed to thoroughly appreciate how lucky we were to have a home in the sun and returning there always gave us an immense feeling of satisfaction and tranquillity. Despite having loved our family home of 31 years this was a completely new way of life, our dream come true.

Together with Bob and Betty and Pauline and Bruce we spent many hours enjoying our new life and meeting new people. We often discussed driving to Portugal.

Plans eventually became reality and we packed our bags and set off in Bob and Betty's people carrier for a week in Albufeira. We did not organise accommodation before setting off. On our arrival Bob left us waiting in his vehicle whilst he made enquiries at a nearby hotel. We were in luck and managed to secure two rooms for the week. We travelled around the area visiting places of interest and enjoying one another's company. The week was over too quickly, and we found ourselves driving along the coast road back to the Costa del Sol. Back home to the life we all loved.

Chapter 9

Over a period of a few years, we made improvements to our apartment and replaced some of the furniture at a local family-owned furniture store.

It was becoming a concern that Ian was beginning to falter quite badly with his memory. He would make light of it and have me laughing at him when he could not remember how to put back together the item he had just dismantled. He drilled holes in the bathroom wall on one occasion to hang a bathroom cabinet and realised too late they were in the wrong place. It was so difficult to witness such mistakes from him knowing how careful he had always been.

On another occasion when decorating the hallway Ian had completely forgotten what he had done, where he was up to and how many coats of paint had gone on! He would get annoyed and argue with me when I tried to help him. It was easier just to let him carry on with what he felt was right. Did it really matter?

Any jobs such as this which had always been an easy task were now becoming fraught with unbelievable problems. It was often better not to start such projects in the first place.

Ian had always been ready and able to carry out most jobs in the home throughout his life, always making satisfactory improvements. His skills as a plumber, decorator, builder, car mechanic, to name but a few, were commendable. It was devastating to see this happening to him.

Thankfully, he was seemingly unaware of his problem and for a while the good days were far more frequent than the bad days.

Chapter 10

We bought a new car in Spain not long after our move in 2007 returning to England to take our other car back for us to use when we were in the UK. The arrangement worked well. The next time we flew into Spain the new car was ready and waiting at the dealership. We took a taxi from the airport and called to collect it to drive home.

Ian's ability to drive had not faltered at all. The only problem was he would forget where he was going. This situation was a difficult one but would be avoided by ensuring there was someone with him giving instructions. I continued to be amazed at his ability to change from driving on the left in the UK to the right in Spain although there was always a little bit of anxiety just in case his memory problem made him forget.

Life is for living and we must get on with it. Not to be held back in any way despite occasional worries I was determined to make the best of what we had but was very much aware of what was happening with Ian's memory problem and it was not going to go away.

Driving in Spain was not something I had ever relished. The thought of it made me somewhat nervous. However, I was very much aware it was quite likely to become a necessity if we were to continue being able to enjoy our life in Spain. We were driving along the coast and Ian was being difficult refusing to pull off an exit to visit the area nearby. He was really annoyed and suddenly pulled off the main road shouting and telling me I would have to drive. I had no option but to take the wheel. The time had come. Not quite the right time, but what must be done, must be done. I took a deep breath and got behind the wheel ensuring Ian was safely in the passenger seat with his seat belt on. No time to practice this was it. If ever there was a time when full concentration was essential it was now. Feeling a little nervous but determined to do this I drove the car into the local area, where we stopped for a relaxing break before venturing back onto the motorway. The trip was a great success. I now felt confident driving in Spain.

It was quite a concern that Ian may have his driving licence withdrawn due to his memory problem. For the moment I preferred to drive, but on occasions Ian had other ideas. Despite his previous annoyance when he insisted that I take the wheel, there were occasions when he did quite the opposite and was adamant that he should drive. He would prise the keys out of my hand. I had no option but to let him drive. Fortunately, our car journeys were normally safe but there was always a lingering worry that it could all go wrong. On a drive to the supermarket in the UK, Ian asked which way now. I told him to take a right at the roundabout ahead. To my utter astonishment he pulled over to turn right immediately in front of the roundabout. My sudden intervention made him realise but he blamed me for the whole scenario. It had been a scary moment.

Back in the UK a few months later Ian had an appointment for a mental ability test which involved puzzles and an actual driving test on the local roads. Waiting for their return from the road test I felt concerned for Ian convinced he would fail. I was expecting an outburst when he was told he could not drive any more. However, this was not the case. He had passed. This was unbelievable. Quite incredible in fact and I was very tempted to query the outcome but realised this would be a difficult task. Questioning the judgement of the examiner and the mental health nurse who accompanied them may not be the way forward. How was I to cope with Ian having already experienced problems which could have caused an accident.

We eventually returned to Spain and life continued in the sun with friends visiting occasionally as well as family. Many magical memories were being made which softened the hard reality of Ian's tragic illness.

Happy times in Spain

Chapter 11

The evidence was there. Ian's memory was deteriorating. Much to my dismay. Our children Roger, Andrew, and Ruth were somewhat concerned. They had many discussions with me about the situation and felt a return to the UK would be beneficial. l was adamant I would know when the time came. For the moment I was hanging on to our little bit of paradise. Ian was happy there and so was I most of the time despite missing our family.

However, travelling to and from the UK had become a trial but was still worth the effort when we got back to our lovely home in the sun. Ian wandered off at the airport and was missing for some time. He needed to use the toilet facilities. I stood by with the hand luggage, but he was a long time. This happened regularly, but he usually returned. What a dilemma on this occasion. Not enough hands to hold the cases and bags, but the need to move to find Ian. There was nothing to do but stand and hope he returned before the flight was called. Ian's bright blonde hair was a good identifier. Suddenly there he was as I scanned the hundreds of faces in the airport lounge. I let go of the bags and waved frantically hoping he would see me. Our eyes met and Ian looked so upset and relieved to find me. I was quite upset too and worried. Shortly afterwards our flight was called.

It was April 2010. We were at the airport waiting for the flight bringing Ruth, Chloe, and Leo to spend a week with us. The weather was currently very warm and sunny. Just nice for a few days around the pool and on the beach. Eating out was always a delight for us all and we particularly enjoyed a lazy morning on the balcony overlooking the pool before driving down to one of the many restaurants for a breakfast. The local pizzeria was a favourite haunt and a nice short walk from the complex if we preferred a walk to driving. The views from there were spectacular. There was nothing better than enjoying a nice meal and a glass of wine or even just calling in for a coffee to sit and relax whilst admiring the view. This was an easy enjoyable life.

Chapter 12

It was early morning, and the phone rang. The voice was initially unrecognisable and sounded quite upset. I soon realised it was Betty. She was distraught having spent the night at the hospital in Marbella with Bob. He had been on life support having suffered a major stroke with devastating consequences and had sadly died. This was terrible news. We had all been out together the previous night for a meal and a few drinks. Bob and Betty had said goodnight and we returned to our apartments. Apparently not long afterwards Bob had begun to feel ill and was talking nonsense. He was displaying all the characteristics of a stroke. Betty contacted their friends Iain and Nancy who had lived in Spain for many years. They came immediately and helped her to get Bob to hospital.

Their lovely life together in their new home was now suddenly cut short. Bob had retired from his building business a few months ago. How could this happen? Everyone was saddened and shocked.

Funerals in Spain are usually held within a few days and Betty and her family decided to proceed with a cremation. Arrangements were made and Betty's family planned to fly out.

For several weeks, a volcano in Iceland had been erupting causing the formation of an ash cloud which began to disrupt flights. All air travel across Western and Northern Europe was cancelled over a period of six days. There were no flights! Many of Bob's relatives and friends were unable to attend his funeral and those who made it before the disruption could not then get a flight home. Everyone who needed a flight was trying desperately to find one. Other means of travel were being investigated and the whole scenario was deadlocked for a while! No-one was going anywhere soon.

At the same time Ruth had to get back to work in the UK and Chloe and Leo to school.

It was the end of their stay, but their flight home was cancelled due to ash cloud. All flights were grounded for several days. Work for Ruth and school for Chloe and Leo should have resumed but they were unable to get home.

One afternoon Ruth was busy searching on her laptop for other means of transport back to the UK. I decided to turn on my laptop too to help her and we began conversing as we searched. After a while Ian seemed to become agitated and was pacing back and forth in the apartment. A few minutes passed by and he approached me and asked me to come into the kitchen. He wanted a word with me. Obligingly I followed him into the kitchen wondering if he was alright. His immediate attitude alarmed me, but I followed him. He was questioning what Ruth and I were doing and what we were talking about and planning. He wanted to know what was going on and why were we being secretive. He thought there was some sort of conspiracy against him hence the agitation. I explained what we were trying to do to get them home, but he remained unconvinced.

Grabbing hold of me he pushed me backwards slamming me into the fridge/freezer. He was staring at me with wide eyes and seemed to be quite aggressive.

He continued to hold me despite my asking him to let go, but he had a tight hold, and I could not move. I let out a scream which immediately brought Ruth running into the kitchen. Seeing the problem, she shouted at her Dad to let go but he turned on her instead grabbing her round the neck and pushing her back into the lounge and over the back of the sofa. I was right behind getting hold of Ian and shouting at him to let go. Chloe was becoming upset by all this. It had to stop. Something seemed to snap in Ian's head like turning off a switch, and thankfully he let go of Ruth and calmed down. A short while later he had no knowledge of his actions even though everyone was still upset.

Eventually a plan of action was put in place to get the family back home. There were other people on the complex needing transport to the UK. Flight attendant Trina and her friend who also needed to get back.

Between them they organised a minibus to drive to Calais to get the ferry.

This had been an upsetting time and I was feeling rather confused and sad. Ruth and the children had had a hard time too.

Once we were on our own again Ian became less agitated and was enjoying the days out and about with just the two of us.

Chapter 13

Betty was now on her own. Since losing Bob she had decided to sell the apartment and return to Scotland to be near her family. The Spanish economy was in decline and unfortunately for those wanting to sell no-one was buying. It was to prove a difficult time for Betty. The flourishing property sales of the past few years had gone downhill. She was going nowhere for the moment and I was determined to ensure she was looked after. The three of us spent a lot of time together enjoying the beach and the local restaurants and sometimes an afternoon doing some retail therapy. We would spend many happy moments at a favourite resort not far away, enjoying a coffee al fresco, then maybe moving on elsewhere for lunch whilst admiring the luxurious boats moored nearby, their owners relaxing on board before moving on to the next port of call.

It had become noticeable how much quieter it was everywhere. Even here people were not moving far. The economy was not in a good place. The beach bars which were usually bursting at the seams were now quiet. The fabulous boats which were still in the marina were going nowhere. Money was scarce. Sad though it was. Cranes hung over the many apartment blocks now motionless. Work had ceased. Nobody was buying any more.

One area which had many apartment blocks under construction was now like a ghost town. Walking around this urbanisation revealed vast areas which were uninhabited. You could hear the occasional conversation coming from a complex which was largely empty with no sign of anyone nearby. Who would want to live like this with un-finished apartment blocks everywhere? Building work was at a complete standstill.

We walked for miles finding new pathways and enjoying the views from the hilltops across the Mediterranean. This was a favourite pastime, but to be done before the intense heat of the day. Meandering along the seafront on the beach, paddling in the sea and having a rest at a favourite beach bar, enjoying lunch before walking back.   In the winter months beaches were empty, and walks were easier. This was ideal being cooler than the height of Summer when walking far was strenuous and hot. Ian was in his element. He was occupied and not inclined to become agitated.

Chapter 14

Ian had been diagnosed with Alzheimer's Disease in 2008 although his memory loss was apparent three or four years previously. Regular appointments with the mental health nurse and the consultant psychiatrist whilst in the UK were keeping him in check. He was taking medication to slow down progress of the disease. However, his aggressive behaviour was becoming more frequent though thankfully it was currently controllable.

This aggressiveness had again been witnessed by family whilst spending a holiday with us at our apartment. Our son Andrew his wife Andrea and our grandchildren, Oliver and Kirsty were enjoying a week with us. I was cooking a meal and Ian was in the kitchen constantly giving me his advice and getting in the way. Andrew was aware that this behaviour from his Dad annoyed me, so he quietly asked him to come and sit down. Unfortunately, Ian was in no mood for a quiet sit down and retaliated by pushing Andrew away quite viciously. Then the fists came into action and Ian began throwing punches. I had to intervene to try to calm the situation.

A short while later whilst I was in the bathroom Ian began banging on the door shouting at me to come out. He sounded agitated but I was not ready to come out needing a few minutes to myself. I told Ian I would be there soon. All went quiet but a few minutes later as I walked into the bedroom, I noticed a shadow behind the shutters on the patio. Suddenly there was a thunderous noise as Ian got hold of the closed shutters and ripped them from the housing. Maybe it was the sound, but whatever it was thankfully Ian calmed down. The shutters needed specialist repair work at a cost. Ian was totally unaware of his actions and remained adamant that he did not break the shutters.

The holiday continued without any further problems until we had planned a day at the beach. This time the problem was nothing to do with Ian. Andrew and family set off to drive to the beach and we would follow in a short while. We took the lift to the basement garage. On opening the heavy fire door into the garage, I could not believe what I was seeing as I looked over to our parked vehicle. Facing me was our lovely new car with what looked like rubble on its roof and bonnet. How had this happened? Where had all that mess come from? There was no rubble in the communal garage. Had someone done this? I had a good idea who it might be. A couple of young Scottish lads renting nearby had taken a dislike to being told not to throw litter in the foyer of our residential block. I was acting president of the resident's association since the demise of Bob who had been president. These lads were troublemakers. Two brothers, who despite living there with their young families had no respect at all for their environment or the other residents. The younger of the two had been witnessed spitting over the balcony of the apartment they were renting. I knew immediately that they were the most likely culprits but had no proof. This kind of behaviour had not happened before until the arrival of these two families.

I needed to let Andrew know what had happened as we would be a bit late, but my hands were shaking so much I struggled to use my mobile phone. Pulling myself together I managed to get hold of Andrew to let him know that we were going to the car wash and would be with them as soon as possible. He was immediately concerned but I managed to convince him that we were sorting the car out and were looking forward to our day at the beach with them.

Not to be deterred from enjoying the day ahead I pressed the button to open the car heading to the car wash having removed most of the cement. On further inspection I found that the door locks had been filled with superglue. It was a good job the doors opened with the remote key. The windscreen wipers had also been stuck down using superglue. However, the car wash fixed most of the mess and before long we were on our way for a day of fun at the beach having calmed down from the initial shock. We got some superglue remover later which released the wiper blades and locks.

Cement and rubble on our car

Ian had remained calm throughout as though the full implications had not sunk in. I was concerned that there could be further trouble. We did not need this, and I was worried that Ian could become aggressive with these two brothers. They had already knocked on our door to talk to me about the complaints against them when they were shouting at me and getting annoyed. I had to keep Ian away as I could see he was ready to take a swipe at them.

After a few anxious months spent keeping an eye on

their activities, which were causing some problems, early one morning the two families were seen loading a van.   They were never seen again but there were many rumours. We were all glad to see the back of them.

Chapter 15

It was late August and l was enjoying a swim in the pool. It was quiet. I was the only one in the pool, but as I swam, I was chatting to my friend Heather on her balcony above. As we talked and I continued my swim, we noticed bits of whiteish grey flakes floating in the air and occasionally into the pool. We began to wonder what it was. The flaky bits continued to come down but neither of us could work out what it was or where it was coming from. I eventually decided it might be a good idea to get out of the pool.

A while later back in the apartment our phone rang. It was Betty ringing to let me know she had heard there was a fire raging in the area and due to the strong wind, it was getting out of control. The police were knocking on doors advising occupants to evacuate their accommodation immediately. Betty told me to go down to the garage with Ian where she would meet us in her car to drive us all down to the bar where we were being told to congregate. I felt panic stricken. Ian was un-aware of the seriousness of the situation and refused to move. He could not understand what was happening. What if the place burned down? Did we need to pack a bag or maybe get the passports out of the safe. There was no time for this, we had to leave. No time to hang around. We must move before it was too late. Betty would be waiting for us. This possibly explained the flakes over the pool. It was obviously ash from a distant fire. But the fire was now much closer. We had to go. I grabbed Ian by the arm despite his objections and we hurried off to find Betty closing our door behind us hopefully not for the last time. As we jumped into Betty's car and came out of the communal garage an alarming sight met us quite close by. We could not have delayed our exit any longer. The fire was indeed raging and spreading at a very rapid rate. It was extremely frightening, and we tried not to panic. We could feel the heat from the flames dancing wildly quite close by. Betty put her foot down and we were soon away from the devastated area wondering if we would ever be able to return.

We arrived at the local bar close to the seafront away from the fire and joined others who were waiting there. It was early evening and darkness was beginning to fall. We could hear the fire engines their bells ringing as they hurried to put out the fire, but it was going to be some time before we could go back to our apartments. As darkness fell the moon turned bright red. It was incredible and unbelievable to see this high in the sky. An alarming sight reflecting the immense fire covering miles of the hillside around the Costa del Sol. A sight I would never forget.

The fire continued to spread and there was no chance we would be allowed back to our apartments for a few hours. It was gone midnight and facilities were made available for those who needed it at the local community hall.

Betty decided to take a ride up the hillside to see what was happening so Ian and I went along too. We found we were unable to go far due to the roadblocks and were quite alarmed to see how close the fire was to the perimeter of our residential complex.

We took advantage of the mattresses in the hall to sleep for a few hours, but l was extremely concerned. I was convinced we would not see our apartment again and was wishing I had at least grabbed our passports before leaving. How were we going to get back to the UK if we lost everything? I eventually fell asleep with this thought going through my head.

Betty had gone across the road to spend some time with

Iain and Nancy who lived nearby. They very kindly made beds available in their apartment for Ian and me to have a rest for a few hours the following morning and provided us with some refreshment too.

After a few hours we heard that people were returning to their homes. This was a great relief but what were we going to find when we got there? The air smelt acrid and was quite strong. It became more pungent the closer we got. However, we were pleasantly surprised and very thankful to find nothing seemed to be damaged. There were one or two windows blown out on the outskirts of the complexes and curtains flapping in the breeze, but on arriving at our apartment it appeared to be intact. There was a lot of cleaning to do due to the ash laying on the patios but that was easily remedied.

The sight that surrounded our apartment block was quite alarming though. The entire area which had once been a haven for the birds and wildlife was now a black landscape as far as the eye could see. The fire had devastated the entire hillside. The trees were black, silhouetted against the skyline and hung over the hillside like something from a horror film. There was no sign of any greenery. It was an unforgiving sight and rather upsetting, but we were lucky to still have our home. Nature would take care of the hillside and the trees and grass would eventually begin to grow again.

It had been a regular Sunday morning walk before breakfast to trek up the hill enjoying the views as we went. Our next walk after the fire proved to confirm that there was nothing left. The rubble pathways were still visible having nothing to burn except the occasional orchid patch which would appear from nowhere. There would be no orchids again for a while. It was an upsetting sight and I felt sad as we returned to our apartment for our breakfast.

Within a few months we were amazed and delighted to see greenery beginning to show here and there. It was quite minimal, but it was there and a wonderful sight to see. Nature is amazing. The hillside was taking shape once again slowly but surely.

Signs of new growth

Chapter 16

In November 2012 we were back in the UK staying with Ruth and family. Whilst shopping in the local supermarket having almost completed our shop Ian told me he felt odd. As he said this, he collapsed holding onto the trolley which tipped over. The weight of it with all the shopping which we had finished, prevented him from crashing to the floor. He was momentarily unconscious but revived quickly and refused an ambulance offered to him by the paramedic who had arrived on the scene. Within a few minutes he was back on his feet. We quickly paid for our shopping and packed it into our car. I was rather concerned about Ian and felt I should take him to hospital, but he seemed reasonably happy and was adamant he did not need to go. However, not long after leaving the car park he passed out again. I pulled over fearing the worst. He was quite pale. I jumped out of the car and opened the passenger door gently lifting Ian's head whilst feeling for his pulse.

Again, within minutes he revived. This was scary and the sooner we got help the better. The house where we were staying with Ruth and family was only a few minutes away and closer than the hospital. On arriving, I jumped out of the car to help Ian inside explaining to our daughter what was happening. She immediately ran inside and dialled the emergency services and the paramedics arrived quickly. Ian passed out again whilst being examined and was taken to hospital. I went in the ambulance with him.

Tests revealed he was suffering from atrial fibrillation and in view of his dementia the best course of action was for him to be fitted with a pacemaker. Unfortunately, the trauma he suffered added further to his already declining prognosis which is often the case in people with dementia.

This new scenario with Ian caused problems when screening at security in the airports. He had to go through a separate gate because of his pacemaker whilst I followed the normal route having to leave Ian to sort himself out. Security staff were made aware of his condition, but he was still my responsibility.

I had to keep a watchful eye on him as best I could whilst ensuring our items were safely back in our bags and pockets and Ian was by my side. It was always a trial, but I persevered.

I was happy that Ian continued enjoying life in a warmer climate being able to spend more time outdoors taking long walks and getting plenty of fresh air. This was also of benefit to me, the climate helping my arthritis and enabling us both to get plenty of exercise.

We returned to Spain after spending a few weeks with our family in the UK having given Ian time to convalesce. Ruth always took us to the airport for our flight and would also pick us up when we returned. On this occasion Ian seemed disorientated and unable to understand what we were doing. He asked me why we were at the airport and seemed happy enough when I explained that we were returning to our apartment for a couple of weeks. Christmas was a few weeks away when we planned to return to spend the festive season with our family as we usually did.

Ian seemed to settle on the flight to Malaga. On our arrival however, he began asking me where we were. Having done this journey many times this was quite un-expected, and I was becoming more and more concerned for him. I kept him close by throughout the train and bus journeys. We arrived at our apartment. It was good to be back there as always. I prepared supper and we spent a couple of hours settling in again when Ian suddenly asked, "where is the toilet?" For a moment I was speechless and thought I must have misheard him. We had been living there for five years. He knew where the bathrooms were. I realised this was quite serious if he could not remember. Since our arrival at the airport Ian had been confused. Had the time come to return to the UK? I did not want to admit it, but the facts were staring me in the face! We could not stay there now if Ian is unable to find his way around the apartment. He seemed to have no idea where he was. He was very confused and upset.

Bedtime was often a trial. Ian sometimes found it difficult to differentiate between his nightwear and his day wear. On occasions he would put his pyjamas on over his other clothes or after putting on his nightwear would then put his trousers and t-shirt back on. I had come to realise over time it was best not to say anything as he would get quite annoyed and aggressive and did it really matter. I did draw the line though at him getting into bed with his shoes on even though getting them off his feet could be a struggle. We were both quite tired and thankfully this time he let me help him and he was in his pyjamas quite quickly and into bed. He wore glasses and normally removed them when getting into bed. However, I noticed he still had them on and quietly told him. He was not happy! Why should he remove them? Further intervention to attempt to remove them made Ian worse. He became agitated. This was not the way forward. Maybe it would be fine if he kept them on. Half an hour later Ian was asleep with his glasses still on though slightly bent. I was still awake having been conscious of the glasses becoming dislodged or broken and causing injury to Ian. I had been unable to sleep. This was the opportunity to try to remove them, so I carefully and gently held them at both sides and took them off to place them on the bedside table. Ian thankfully remained asleep, and I could now relax and sleep too.

Chapter 17

On waking the first thought I had was not a happy one and I felt rather sad and upset at what lay ahead. We must return to England to be with our family and get help for Ian. He needed to be accessible to the mental health team who had been monitoring him during the progression of his condition. It was no longer beneficial to Ian for us to remain in Spain.

On speaking to our children, they had no hesitation agreeing with my decision. No doubt they were relieved to hear that we were coming back to live in the UK, and they were all ready to help me with the move. Christmas was only a few days away. In the meantime, sadly I began the process of putting in place the measures required to sell our property and arrange for the removal of our furniture to England. We started collecting boxes to pack all our belongings in. There was a lot to clear from the apartment.

The days that followed were fraught with worry. Keeping a close eye on Ian and making plans for our forthcoming move kept me rather busy. However, all was going well, and a few items not needed for our current stay in the apartment could be packed into the boxes. It was going to be a tight schedule. The move was set for the end of January. We would have three days with the family returning to Spain with Ian and I to complete all the packing. The removals company had been organised. Our flight back was timed to depart a few hours after the removals van left with our home on board. Hopefully, it would all be on schedule.

I had to decide what to do about our car. Whilst discussing this with the agents selling our property, I was delighted to learn that they were interested in buying it. We had known them since living there and knew it would be going to a good home. I took them to the garage so they could inspect the car and a price was soon agreed with the unexpected bonus of a cash sale.

The car would be handed over in a few days. The move and all arrangements were going very well.

Chapter 18

During a quiet moment thinking about the past few years in Spain and how much we had enjoyed it; I began reflecting on the amazing insight our children had several years ago and the exciting trip they organised as a surprise for us in 2002. It would certainly not be possible now. It was part of our plans when we were retired and had time on our hands.

Back then it was coming up to Ian's 60th birthday. I had discussed with our family that I was planning a special surprise for him. I wanted family and close friends to join us for a celebratory dinner at an hotel on the outskirts of Chester. We were both James Bond fans. I had the idea of telling Ian it was to be a James Bond themed evening so that he would dress accordingly in his tuxedo and be ready for the special dinner laid on in his honour. He believed the evening and weekend was just for us to celebrate together. He had no idea all the family and a few friends would be there too.

We set off on our journey to Chester enjoying a relaxing drive stopping on the way for a light lunch. I took the opportunity whilst visiting the ladies' room to let family and friends know we were on our way and would be arriving in approximately half an hour. The plan went accordingly, and Ian suspected nothing. He was looking forward to a special weekend to celebrate his 60th birthday with me. We checked in at reception and were given the key to our room. This was exciting and Ian was totally unaware family and friends were quietly waiting inside. He put the key in the door not suspecting at all. There was complete quiet until, surprise, surprise! Ian walked into the room seeing all the smiling faces of everyone waiting to welcome him and celebrating loudly. There was a lot of clapping and party poppers and everyone began to sing Happy Birthday. He was looking quite shocked and amazed. This was such a special memorable occasion.

The next part of the evening celebrations was even more of a surprise. Not just for Ian but for me too. After a very enjoyable meal and a toast for Ian's 60th Ruth stood up and passed some pictures to Ian and me telling us we had to guess what the pictures were. The first one was a Koala bear. Why did we need to guess it was obvious what it was? As more pictures were given to us, we suddenly realised there was a theme. All the pictures were associated with Australia. Unbelievably this was the gift of a lifetime from our children. They were sending us on a fabulous holiday to Australia, Bali, and Singapore. This was for my 60th too which would be in 2004.

During our scuba diving years, we had often mentioned how we would love to dive on the Great Barrier Reef. This was now to become a reality. They had thought of everything. We were booked on the quicksilver catamaran which would take us out to Agincourt reef. A smorgasbord luncheon was to be enjoyed on board before departure. We could not wait to go.

A Photo by TW

Chapter 19

Back to reality and what lay ahead. First though, I looked forward to a nice break spending a few weeks back in the UK for the Christmas holidays with our family before moving out of our lovely home, our "little bit of paradise" in late January.

Travelling was always a problem now and becoming more so with the passage of time. Ian had to be constantly watched to ensure he did not wander off. Simple routine tasks such as needing to use the toilet facilities was not something I could do and leave Ian on his own. Neither could Ian use the male facilities on his own. I was unaware at this stage of Ian's illness that we could have used the disabled facility. Many of the disabled toilets were only accessible with a key which could be obtained from the local authority at a small charge, providing you had a valid reason. This would certainly have made our outings much easier. There had been many anxious moments when Ian was missing for some time and I had to ask the men coming out if they had seen anyone who fitted Ian's description. Thankfully, he had always turned up eventually. Goodness knows what he had been doing all the time he was missing. This ongoing problem made me realise that our planned move was essential. We had been lucky enough to travel to many places over the years.

Christmas with our family was very enjoyable. A busy time buying and wrapping presents, decorating the Christmas tree, and preparing the food for everyone. A delightfully magical time too with our grandchildren who were so excited for what lay ahead when Santa came with their presents.

A priority for me to deal with was to find somewhere to live and I had been looking at flats to rent in the area close to Ruth and family. Our furniture would be arriving as soon as we were able to give the removalcompany our address. We managed to find suitable accommodation and could now relax and enjoy the festive season.

New Year was celebrated with an evening at an Indian restaurant which ended with a brilliant firework display as the bells rang out to welcome the new year.

A few weeks into January and it was nearing time to return to Spain to complete the packing and empty the apartment ready for the return to England. Ian and I flew back with our three children, Roger, Andrew, and Ruth, together with our grandson Leo who was now eight years old. We had three days before the flight back. It was a very hectic time but with help from everyone we were ready for the removals van to collect all the boxes and furniture on the last day. The situation was surreal. Five years since the start of living our dream that dream now had to end but at least we had done it. Sadly, Ian seemed totally unaware of what was happening. He remained quiet throughout never once asking any of us what we were doing and why.

Closing the door for the last time was hard. It was the oddest feeling giving up our lovely home in the sun, and I had an overwhelming feeling of sadness.

Everyone was feeling low, but we had to get on with our journey to the airport and board the flight back to the UK. We took one last look around at the place we all loved, where we had enjoyed many happy moments. It was so awfully sad leaving Betty behind, but she had other friends until she sold her apartment and moved back to Scotland. Our goodbyes were hard, but we planned to meet up regularly when Betty eventually returned to her home in West Lothian.

Our flight was un-eventful. We were all deep in thought about the events of the last few days and feeling relieved that it had all worked out. We were soon back and getting on with our lives. The next step for Ian and I was to move into the apartment as soon as the removals company could schedule our furniture and boxes. In the meantime, we would be staying with Ruth and family. Ruth's job often took her away from home and we were always happy to be there and care for our grandchildren.

Chapter 20

We moved in to our 2 bedroomed flat in the middle of January. Our furniture had arrived safely from Spain and was delivered and installed. The gradual process of putting everything in place was beginning.

Ian was becoming less aware of situations as time progressed. He was of little assistance in my time of need but obviously this could not be helped. He had an illness. My attempts to talk to him to try to find what his opinion was on various matters proved difficult. It would have been helpful on occasions to have Ian's opinion. He was quite adamant throughout that he did not have a memory problem. I dearly wanted him to discuss this memory problem with me in the hope it would help him, but it was not to be.

On one occasion when I tried to prove to him that he could not remember I asked him what my name was. There was complete silence as he stared at me. I hoped any minute he would say my name, but he said nothing. He just continued looking at me then suddenly blurted out "I don't know". I felt disgusted with myself for making him face his problem. I also felt so sad he no longer knew my name. I need not have worried that this would upset Ian. Within minutes he had forgotten the incident. But I would go on to remember it forever.

We got on with our life attending regular appointments to monitor Ian and enjoying time with our family.

Our flat was adequate but not really where I wanted to stay for too long. It was an old building and in need of some attention with quite small rooms but sufficed for the time being until we could find somewhere better. I began looking around in the same area for a more modern place with better facilities.

After six months we moved to a larger more modern apartment.

It can be very confusing for dementia patients to change their surroundings and I was concerned moving around would upset Ian.

On this occasion I had more time to make a choice and hoped this move would be our last for some time.

Our family visited us regularly and child minding at our daughters became a regular routine where we would stay overnight. Ian seemed happy enough and was familiar with the surroundings there having stayed many times. It did however concern me a bit because he was no longer capable of retaining information in his memory. He was still driving but I it did bother me somewhat. There had been minor upsets when he seemed unsure and his awareness of measurements when assessing a parking space was becoming impaired. He needed constant reminders of where he was going and had to be given instruction all the time. Having passed the test undertaken a few months previously, I felt I had no chance of convincing Ian he was not fit to drive although he probably did not remember having taken it with the mental health assessor accompanying him whilst I had to wait at the unit. Tactics had to be devised to ensure that I was the driver which was not an easy task.

Ian was attending regular check-ups with the consultant psychiatrist to monitor the progression of the disease. It became obvious during the routine procedure that his co-ordination and mental ability had deteriorated and would not be conducive to him driving. The consultant had no alternative but to inform the DVLA. I felt upset but was also much relieved. To my surprise there was no adverse reaction from Ian. He did not say a word.

Chapter 21

In January 2013, I found out that the Alzheimer's Society ran a caring and coping course for people looking after someone with dementia so I decided this might help with my understanding of Ian's condition and enable me to help him. It proved to be very fruitful. Nonetheless it was quite distressing to learn of the consequences of the disease and how it progressed, together with the anticipated lifespan of patients. The disease is of course incurable. However, attending the course led to the discovery of classes for people with dementia and their carer and Ian and I started going to singing for the brain, boccia (bowling for the disabled), dancing and various other groups. These classes were all quite beneficial and we made many friends who were going through similar problems. Getting together for an hour or two of social fun and games was enjoyable.

As a result of the course to gain a better understanding of coping with Alzheimer's Disease, a carers' café was organised between those of us wishing to continue to meet when the course finished. It became a fortnightly social meeting at a local garden centre café. The meetings had become a welcome part of our lives. We enjoyed our get togethers which gave us a couple of hours of relief from the stresses and strains of caring for someone. The group helped one another through difficult times too when it was necessary. Our experiences were called upon occasionally when new members needed help and advice. We also organised short breaks together which took us to see shows in London and enjoy days out and about for a change from the usual itinerary. A trip to Liverpool to follow the trail of the Beatles, was a memorable event and we all got on well enjoying our time together.

Ian was quite happy to spend time on his own at this stage and I felt it was safe for him to be left. I would leave him a large note detailing my whereabouts and my mobile number in case he forgot where I had gone which he invariably did. I had done this several times, but a niggling doubt about his safety was beginning to creep in. This was unfortunately confirmed when I returned from my outing to the carers' café one day to find Ian toasting a slice of bread by holding it over the gas burner on the hob. I was alarmed at the implications of this and told Ian it was not good practice. He told me he had already had one slice and it was perfect. This incident had occurred at our daughter's home. Ruth and I were both concerned knowing the problems caused by Ian's illness. He needed supervision for the times when I was out, or I did not go.

It had been recognised by the social care team, together with the psychiatric nurse who visited Ian regularly for a progress report, that a session of respite care would probably be beneficial. He began attending two days a week at a local health centre for five hours. I was able to take him and collect him getting some relief myself in between and Ian was kept occupied, along with other patients. The mental health team kept them all happy with various activities, tea, and cake on arrival and a nice substantial lunch. It was a good arrangement for us both.

Our lives were full of routine now which was good for Ian and helpful to me. I looked forward to having a bit of time to myself and felt it was helpful to Ian doing tasks and enjoying the social side of being with patients and staff at the care centre.

Life was easier for the moment. We were making the best of having to live back in the UK although I missed our "little bit of paradise" in Spain.

Chapter 22

We were sitting at home enjoying a few hours relaxing together on the sofa on a beautiful Summer's day, having had a lovely walk taking in the gentle breeze, the blue sky, and the warm sunshine. Suddenly in just a few words the enjoyment of the afternoon became a blur. Ian was asking me "what are all those people doing in the hall?" Did I hear him correctly? My mind was buzzing. What did he say? What people? How did they get into our home? I was certain I had locked the door as I always did. I turned my head away from Ian and looked toward the hall expecting to see people wondering how they got in to our flat. I was feeling quite worried and scared! There was no-one there, no-one at all. How could this be? Was this my loving husband sitting next to me? What were those words he said? Sudden realisation and my heart beats faster. I have an incredible feeling of utter devastation. Ian really believed there were people in the hall. I had a sudden urge to shake him and make him come to his senses. He had a strange expression on his face. His eyes were staring watching the people in the hall. I had an overwhelming feeling of sadness. This was real. I was not dreaming. Ian suddenly became more agitated still seeing people. I must do something quickly to relieve the situation. I immediately changed the subject attempting to distract him. "Shall we have a cup of tea? Come and help me make it". I gently grabbed Ian's hand and we walked toward the kitchen. In just a moment my actions have focussed his attention on another matter. We enjoyed our cup of tea. For now, thank goodness the people have gone! All is quiet again.

It is becoming more obvious with the passage of time and a better understanding of the experiences with Ian and his deterioration, that Alzheimer's Disease is unbelievably horrendous. I find it difficult to believe that Ian is beginning to hallucinate. Seeing people in the hall served to confirm this. I feel incredibly sad and upset at what is happening to him. This is the man who is the love of my life and means everything to me.

Alzheimer's is a blanket of darkness slowly closing over the mind. It will suddenly escalate for a while changing the person into someone you no longer know.

Life was becoming a mystery for me. It was certainly a challenge learning how to deal with circumstances beyond my control. Every day had its ups and downs. There was no normality to life now? What would today bring? What would tomorrow bring? Ian had no control over his body and his mind. He would be devastated if he knew what I was having to deal with. There was no privacy and no embarrassment on his part because he had no understanding. Emotions were running high, and I was up one minute and down the next. Deciding about Ian's care was not easy. Would it be the right decision I had to make when having to deal with events in our lives which I never expected to experience. My dear husband would speak to me as though I was a stranger, as though I had no knowledge of him and his achievements.

It was so hurtful. The acceptance of this was unbearably difficult and not something to dwell on. Throughout all this I must try to focus on all the good times, the years that have gone whilst holding on to all the wonderful memories. I must do my utmost to hang on to those memories. They are to be treasured. Life goes on and I must make the best of it, take a deep breath, and move on even though at times it feels futile and worthless. Life is precious to the very last thread.

Learning how to deal with situations that have never arisen

before can be fraught with dilemmas. The aggression shown by Ian puts me in an exceedingly difficult position when trying to make the right decision to diffuse these potentially dangerous moments. I can feel the anger rising in me and an urge to punch him and hurt him back is overwhelming as he uses all his strength to prevent me from moving. I must overcome the anger! I feel trapped by the man who has been the love of my life for almost 50 years, my lifelong friend the father of our three amazing children and grandpa to our adorable grandchildren. Where did he go? The need to have him back is pulling at my heartstrings. I hang on to every hour of every day hoping my man will come back to me.

Identifying when fireworks are about to commence causes feelings of panic, but I must hold it together and be assertive. Change the subject and hope it works. Keep calm and not get angry.

We had been living with dementia for several years now although looking back I did not recognise the symptoms and thought it was simply memory loss. Having to make decisions was something we always discussed, and such discussions had never been a problem in our lives, but now I was the decision maker and always hoped they were the right decisions.

Alzheimer's Disease had robbed us of our idyllic life in Southern Spain and a large amount of money was lost selling our Spanish home at a time when the economy was bad. That phase of our lives was behind us now and completely eradicated from Ian's memory. I was grateful to have had that time and fulfil our dream of spending months and years living in the sun. It did happen.

With the passage of time an understanding of coping with dementia was beginning to evolve. However, the frustrations still lingered on. Recognising, and avoiding this became an art which would help relieve a situation. I related it to managing the relationship as if handling a child and allowing more time to prepare. I had another person as well as myself to consider. He needed guidance and consideration. It was all too easy to forget this fact and become stressed due to the pressure. I tried to remember to always handle him with care. He is an adult and sad to say he has an illness.

I gave myself a slap now and again. Attempts to keep to a daily routine could become fraught with anxiety and I often felt inadequate and helpless. This state of mind did not give positive signals. Tears require an explanation and how do you explain such feelings without causing even more anxiety and distress. I must put on a brave face whenever possible. It was hard to cope with the problems which arose due to this progressive illness. It was a daily struggle to cope with my own needs and requirements as well as the extended responsibilities I now had every day. Forgetting appointments had never been a problem in the past. However, I realised I too am getting older and could do without all these additional problems at this time of my life. I must not beat myself up but try to be positive.

We still occasionally laughed at ourselves.

There were some rather hilarious moments and times when Ian was quite lucid and seemed to understand. For example, whilst bringing the car to a halt at our destination I got out waiting for Ian to do the same, but I noticed he seemed to be struggling with his seat belt. Walking round to open the passenger door to help him I could see he had fastened his coat over the top of the seat belt and could not work out what he had done. When he realised what he had done he laughed.

At home we had a resident poltergeist which regularly hid items some of which have never reappeared. It was ridiculous.

Conversations were often quite bizarre and caused me to laugh at the impossible and incomprehensible discussions I had with Ian. The fly on the wall would be laughing too.

Chapter 23

Improving our lives and trying to help Ian as much as possible with his problem were quite important to me. Lightening the load for a while with distractions from the daily routine and enjoying the company of others letting the problems float away for a few hours was a great asset. It was much harder to return to equilibrium when on a downward spiral. I realised I must not let that happen and not dwell on the demons but look forward to brighter times. Those brighter times had certainly enhanced our lives.

Attending singing for the brain which was held every week and focussed on music enjoying a sing song with others, was a tonic for both of us. Similarly, the dance café which was held once a month was a few hours of socialising helping Ian to dance. It was unbelievable how he had forgotten to dance especially as he had always been a wonderful dancer. He now needed encouragement and instruction to do what would have previously been routine.

The local psychiatric nurse called to see Ian at our home from time to time to check and assess him casually. He also attended six monthly consultations with a psychiatrist when routine tests were undertaken to calculate any deterioration. It had become quite clear over a period of several years that the prognosis was not good. Ian's memory was in decline. The test results were lower than the last time. I was relieved on the occasions when the score remained constant.

Ian continued to go to respite care twice weekly at the health centre within walking distance of our home. Walking there occasionally he would decide he did not want to go. It reminded me of the time when our children did not want to go to nursery and would get upset. We always got there eventually with a little bit of persuasion. I would go to the gym or for a nice swim whilst I had the opportunity.

Our lives revolved around Ian's illness and I was very much aware that his aggression was becoming more of a concern. I remained vigilant in my attempts to keep him calm when situations arose which could escalate.

He had taken to staring out of the windows of our apartment when one day, out of the blue he told me he was looking for his Mum and would occasionally mention his Dad too. I learned quickly not to say to him that his parents died several years ago. This would cause him to respond violently. He continued to be adamant they were still alive and lived nearby. I would often say to myself is this really happening. It was so hard.

Chapter 24

One afternoon in midsummer when I was about to start preparing our eening meal, Ian was looking out of the window and suddenly said he was going out to see his Mum. He was convinced she lived in a house he could see from the window across the road on a new housing estate. I tried to keep calm and asked him to wait for a little while and I would go with him. However, he was not waiting, and immediately headed down the stairs to the main door before I could stop him. He grabbed the door handle to open it. The door was locked. He had begun wandering out of the apartment occasionally and to prevent this I kept the door locked and removed the key. Because he could not get through the door he was annoyed and upset and began shouting at me to open it. By now he had come back up the stairs to find me for the key and grabbed hold of me to come and unlock the door. He almost toppled me and himself down the stairs in his attempt to get out to find his Mum. By now I was shaking. What a dilemma. If I did not let him through the door what would happen? I had to open the door, but this was not good either. Ian was determined he was going. What was I to do? The more I delayed the angrier Ian became. There was no time to think. He was becoming more and more aggressive. I felt I had no alternative but to open the door. He ran straight out as the door flew open. I stood frozen to the spot watching him go and finding it hard to believe what was happening. I could not move despite telling myself to go after him. Fear had taken hold of me. It was like a bad dream and I would wake up soon. I was having too many bad dreams recently. I came to my senses and panicked. Quickly. Ian had gone. I had to move and go to look for him. He could hurt himself or someone else. Where had he gone? I ran into the street and across the road to the building site that Ian had been looking at from the window. There was no sign of him and no-one around to ask. My mind was buzzing.

What should I do? Where should I go? Ian could be anywhere. He may have gone in a different direction. I ran back home and grabbed the car keys, jumped in my car, and set off to find Ian searching frantically in every street nearby and driving in every direction. I was really scared. Scared what could happen to Ian. He could be anywhere. He would have no idea how to get home. But what was I doing driving round and round? Twenty minutes had passed. Ian could be anywhere! I needed to get help. I told myself this was not a good idea and to calm down and ring the police. Driving straight back home I hoped Ian would be there, but he was not at home. I must do something before it was too late. As I entered our flat, I could hear the answerphone beeping. I grabbed the phone to listen, and the message was from the receptionist at our doctor's surgery saying she thought they had my husband there and could I go as soon as possible to identify him. I could not get there quickly enough. Hurrying into the surgery I spotted Ian immediately. What a relief. He was looking very distressed but obviously recognised me. A young man was with him. He had been working on the building site when he had noticed Ian wandering around getting upset. He realised the dilemma and very sensibly took Ian to the surgery. I told the young man how grateful I was and thanked him very much for his presence of mind. We were immediately taken in to see the doctor. He talked to us for a while about the situation and then suggested I take Ian home and make him a cup of tea. Feeling thankful I left the surgery with Ian and headed home. He enjoyed his cup of tea and I gave him one of the tablets to relieve his aggression and psychosis. He had no recollection of the incident when I tried to discuss it with him. Maybe this was a good thing.

Sitting on the sofa, watching the TV in the early evening Ian went over to the window again. My heart sank and I was immediately concerned and anxious. I watched him closely and within a few minutes he said he was going out. As before I told him to wait a few minutes and I would go with him. In that moment, the telephone rang. I answered and it was our son Roger. To my relief Ian sat down on the sofa. Roger had been working and had just heard what happened to Ian earlier in the day. He was ringing to talk to me about it. I immediately told Roger that Ian was getting agitated again and wanted to go out looking for his Mum. Roger told me to put him on the phone. I passed the phone to Ian and he sat back and relaxed listening to what Roger had to say. The tablet I gave Ian earlier was probably beginning to take effect too. Talking on the phone was helping a lot and making Ian focus on something else. He started to become quite sleepy, and I took hold of the phone to tell Roger I had to get Ian to bed before he fell asleep on the sofa. The potentially hazardous situation had been averted for now, thank goodness.

Chapter 25

The following day was not a good one. I had a decision to make and did my best to postpone what I knew was my only option. The psychiatric nurse had been informed of the problems with Ian going off on his own to look for his Mum. She was aware that Ian's aggressiveness was getting worse and had a suggestion to make. She had had to make a quick exit herself on her last visit when Ian got annoyed with her and began using threatening behaviour. There was a bed available for Ian at a mental health unit so that he could be assessed and to give me some respite from caring for him. Although I hated to admit it, he was becoming difficult to handle and a danger to both himself and me. It was a terrible dilemma for me. I dd not want him to go into a home but his condition had reached a stage where medication was necessary to calm him, and this needed to be done in a controlled environment with nursing care to assess his requirements and determine the correct amount of medication required to give the desired effect. My initial reaction was to try coping with him at home for a few more days or weeks. I absolutely hated the idea of him being in a home. This was not what I planned for him. Maybe I needed to change my tactics and try harder to prevent Ian becoming aggressive. Maybe it was my fault. However, the nurse expressed her concerns. Ian could wander off again and cause untold problems. He may even attack me with disastrous results or even a member of the public if he went walkabout again. He was at a great risk of being harmed himself too when wandering the streets.

The nurse also said to me that the weekend was approaching when help was not as readily available should I need it. Also, the bed would probably be taken as there were other patients in need of this facility. Under the circumstances I had no alternative but to accept the bed for Ian.

This had been coming for a while and although I knew it had to happen it was not a happy situation and I had kept putting it to the back of my mind.

Packing Ian's case with his belongings was awful. It all felt surreal. I was wandering around in a daze and feeling terribly guilty to be organising his place in a home. What did I need to pack for him? How could I do this to the man I adored and always looked forward to spending time with. It was heart breaking. We had spent little time apart throughout the years since we first met as teenagers. Everything we did, we did together, and I was finding it hard to believe that Ian did not question my actions. They were his clothes going into the case and none of mine. Why was he not asking me why I was packing a case with his things? Sadly, he was totally unaware of what was happening. He was not capable of assessing situations and querying them. This only served to prove that he needed further help which I was not able to provide for him at home much as I had tried. It was all so very upsetting. I felt as though I had failed him.

Ian had already been attending the respite care centre once a week before his condition had deteriorated and was familiar with the building and the staff but whether he remembered it all was indeterminable. I was never sure what he remembered and what he did not. There were signs sometimes that he understood and remembered but he was unable to communicate this to anyone. He had been transferred from the local health centre to be under the control of the psychiatric nursing team so they could administer the required medication.

The drive to the home was not an easy one. Ian did not question where we were going. Although I had done the journey several times before, this felt entirely different. Another stage of Ian's dementia treatment was about to begin.

The staff at the home were expecting Ian and took him straight to his room so that I could unpack his belongings and settle him in. It was a very upsetting time, and I was finding it hard to concentrate on what I was doing. I felt quite desperate and did not want to leave Ian and go home to an empty apartment. However, I really did not have a choice. I was extremely upset.

This was the beginning of another chapter and I felt genuinely concerned about the future and not being able to enjoy my remaining years with my loving husband. I fully intended to spend as much time with Ian as possible, visiting him at the home as often as I could. There were many times when I just wanted to take him home with me.

Alzheimer's Disease is unforgiving and relentless turning the sufferer into someone you no longer know.

Chapter 26

Ian's aggressiveness became worse over the next few weeks. He began trying to get out of windows in the home and through doors by kicking them. The doctor at the home decided to review Ian's situation and I was called in to discuss the best way forward with the team looking after him. It was quite distressing to learn they were recommending Ian be detained under the deprivation of liberty safeguards. The circumstances for this decision were explained and were being put in place for Ian's safety and in his interests. There was no alternative but to agree to this procedure, but it made me feel so desperate for his well-being. This was not at all what I wanted to hear. I was instantly reminded of my discussion with Ian several years ago when his memory had become a concern, suggesting he should see his doctor. His reaction at the time had been quite disturbing and upsetting and the deprivation of liberty was a similar scenario to being sectioned. I could not help but feel Ian may believe I have purposely done this, and he was in no position for me to be able to explain it all to him. Sadly, I could no longer communicate with him. I was devastated but had to put this out of my mind. It was likely that events years ago were no longer part of Ian's memory, but I would never know the answer.

Visits to spend time with Ian were now a daily routine. I hoped he was aware I was there for him and on occasions a glimmer of recognition seemed to show, but not always. We would sometimes enjoy a meal together and I was happy to see Ian eating well. He still enjoyed his food. We would sit together in the lounge with other patients and relatives. It was always difficult to leave. Sometimes Ian would try to follow me when he knew I was leaving. Staff would always distract him. Not a happy situation for either of us. I always felt I wanted to take him with me and how awful it was to leave him there.

The tears would flow as I left him behind.

Reading through Ian's review from the home was quite harrowing. Although I was fully aware of my husband's problems seeing it written down on an official document highlighted the full facts and they were hard to read. I felt as though it was all a bad dream and hoped I would wake up soon and find him there beside me at home. My loving husband full of fun and enjoying life. But this was not to be.

Some days were good, some days were bad. On the bad days when I went to spend time with Ian, he would be difficult. There were times when he wandered around the home seemingly not at all aware that I was there. On other occasions he would be more pleasant, sitting with me for long periods but there was no conversation. Ian's cognitive impairment prevented him being able to communicate but I did my best to chat to him and would play music on my phone for him to listen to or read to him from a book, magazine, or newspaper in the hope I would get him to react.

Ian had always enjoyed playing his guitar. In his youth he had been a member of a group of 3 lads who played pop music together at various social events. I decided to take his guitar to the home and attempt to get him to play. However, my efforts were unrewarded. He seemed to have lost the ability to play and it was upsetting. On one occasion however, when Roger was visiting, he sat on the bed with his Dad and put the guitar on his lap. Ian managed to strum a little and this was heartening to everyone and lifted Ian's spirits too. It brought smiles all round.

Now that Ian was detained in a home, I could no longer go to the social events we had been attending, organised by the Alzheimer's Society for dementia patients and their carer's. Our places were needed for others. There was quite a waiting list as this was a popular pastime. Singing for the brain had been a life saver for us both and a thoroughly enjoyable couple of hours on a Monday afternoon. As Ian's condition worsened it had become difficult to get him in and out of the car and he was prone to falling asleep and did not join in with our singing.

On one occasion he did not respond at all when it was time to go home. He would not move from his chair and seemed to be in a daze. A colleague who had a wheelchair in his car kindly brought it to get Ian out, but moving him from the chair proved to be a huge challenge. He was not moving no matter what I did to try to encourage him. With assistance I had to lift him from his chair into the wheelchair. The same problem occurred when attempting to get Ian into the car. It was becoming troublesome and upsetting and no longer of any benefit to Ian or me, sad though it was.

Chapter 27

A few days enjoying a break in Scotland was of great benefit to me although I felt quite guilty not being able to visit Ian for a few days. The trip had been booked some time ago for Ian and me to enjoy a few days away together. In his absence our granddaughter Kirsty, accompanied me. It was a coach holiday and a chance to relax and be taken to various interesting places. It was nice to spend a few days with Kirsty and I enjoyed her company.

Returning home, I was shocked to hear that Ian had innocently caused quite an incident at the home. The staff had been unable to locate him despite searching everywhere. They assumed he had got out through the security door. When he did not turn up after some time, it had become necessary to involve the police and a search of the local area had been undertaken. Ian was quite safe. He was found completely oblivious to the frantic search going on for him and was quite happily sitting in a chair inside the home. The staff had informed Ruth that her dad was missing, and she had contacted her brothers to let them know the situation. They had decided not to alert me knowing I would probably panic and feel I should come home. Thank goodness Ian was safe.

Visits to see him had become a regular routine. Keeping a check on him taking him sweets, cake, and drinks to brighten his day helped me to get through the days, weeks, and months without him at home. He was struggling to adjust and caused one or two problems which were quite worrying. The first home he was admitted to was mixed gender patients. Ian could be quite aggressive on occasions reacting badly to situations which would have normally been routine. He was prone to invading the space of other patients and causing an upset. It was eventually decided to transfer him to a male only environment. I was called to the home to discuss the way forward. It was all very un-settling and distressing and I hoped this transfer would help Ian. He seemed to be struggling with adjusting but that could be due to his illness.

The first visit to see Ian in the new home was quite worrying. Before I was allowed into the area with the patients, I was handed a panic alarm and shown how to use it. I was quite shocked that this should be necessary. Ian was in the main lounge area quite happily sitting in a comfy chair enjoying a cup of tea and a biscuit. I sat down beside him desperately hanging on to the panic alarm just in case. There were a few patients around but there was no indication if any of them were likely to become violent or cause trouble. Until I got to know them all a bit better it was sometimes difficult to differentiate between patients and visitors. The panic alarm was not needed.

However, on occasions I did have to deal with patients. One man was always looking for his sister and asked if I had seen her and would she be coming to visit him. I gradually learned how to deal with him, but it was sometimes quite difficult and worrying. There were incidents when patients began fighting. Staff were usually around and carried panic alarms. I was on my way into the home one day when I was grabbed around the wrist by a patient who I knew could be a problem. I had witnessed one or two events where the staff had to deal with him using their panic alarms to call for assistance. He would not let go of me which was very scary as there were no staff in the immediate area. I told myself not to panic as this would only make the situation worse. Delaying tactics were necessary. Chatting to him and trying to keep him calm I was relieved when help came, and he let go. He had a tight hold around my wrist throughout and there was no way I was getting out of it. Relieved that help had arrived after what had seemed like a long time, I went to find my husband and spend a couple of hours with him.

Ruth visited her Dad too when she was able as did Roger and Andrew, but they all had their work commitments. They were all keeping in touch with the situation, and I updated them regularly. They were always invited to the meetings held with the staff and social services to discuss Ian's care and the way forward for him. It was helpful and comforting for me to have them along to give me their support. We all found it hard to believe what was happening.

Tony, Ian's friend of many years going back to their youth when they were in the air training corps together, would visit Ian as often as he could, despite living in Newark for many years, a fair distance to travel. Tony was a good friend to me too. I had also known him for many years since we were 11 years of age. We lived close to one another and attended the same Sunday school.

Chapter 28

I was reasonably happy and kept myself busy taking time to look after my grandchildren in Ruth's absence. There was no point dwelling on the unhappy situation with Ian, but it was always there at the back of my mind. I had to do my utmost to keep myself fit and well to be there for him, but also as my family kept telling me I had to have a life myself.

Ian continued to receive residential nursing care, but his bouts of aggressiveness were proving difficult to handle. I was called in for a meeting with staff again. On this occasion I was shocked to hear that he was to be transferred to Billingham Grange, Stockton-on-Tees. My initial feelings were that he would be too far away for me to visit him and I felt upset not wanting this for either of us. This could not happen. I needed to see him regularly and keep an eye on his care. On discussing it with staff who travelled there regularly to assess patients, I realised it was only about 40 miles away from my home and therefore, not too far. I decided it would be more sensible to visit Ian a few times a week for longer periods.

I began visiting Ian at Billingham Grange after giving him a few days to settle into his new surroundings as I was requested to do. I found I quite enjoyed the drive. It was straightforward once I had been and found the way. I used my satnav which helped me a lot when going somewhere new. Sometimes I would call at the shopping precinct opposite the home and buy a daily newspaper to read. Ian loved a packet of crisps now and again and maybe some chocolate and a can of pop. I had noticed how his tastes had changed in recent months. He had more of a sweet tooth now and enjoyed jelly and ice cream occasionally, a dessert he would have declined prior to his illness. At least his appetite continued to be good.

Some days I would have lunch with Ian which was always enjoyable. I looked forward to spending time with him and would feel quite excited to see him again as I got nearer to the home. The staff would bring us a plate of sandwiches and a tea or coffee.

There were comfortable lounge areas where families and friends could sit and relax together. All three of our children would visit as often as they could and on occasions our grandchildren came along too.

There were games to play and books to read, none of which were of interest to Ian, but he did find a ball and made me laugh when he would not throw it to me. I patted the ball attempting to get him to throw it and he started to smile so I did it again. It was quite funny and had instigated a reaction which was remarkable. He was not letting go of the ball though.

As Ian's treatment progressed, he would often be very sleepy. I was always quite sad when I found him fast asleep after a long drive to see him. I would talk to him hoping he would wake up but often there was no response. He was not waking up. Ruth occasionally took me in her car, and we would find him sleeping when we got there. Despite staying a while, sadly we eventually left having failed to wake him. A similar thing happened too when Tony visited him, having driven to York from Newark first. It was extremely hard to leave without having a chance to communicate with Ian. Tony had come a long way but what could we do? Ian could be sleeping for a while. l was never sure if Ian knew I was there. When he was awake, he did seem to respond and was happy to sit with me but did not know who I was or who else was there to spend time with him. He did however, surprise me one day when I told him Tony was coming to visit. I got a response and was astonished to hear him say "TW". Tony's initials. This response made me realise he had understood what I said to him. It was amazing. However, he had never called Tony "TW" in all the years we had been friends so where did that suddenly come from? Ian gave me a cheeky grin as he said it which made it even more intriguing. What was going on in his head?

What followed was extremely harrowing for me and our family. Ian seemed to be deteriorating despite an improvement in his aggression which was now under control. He would often seem very distant and unable to communicate at all. The balance of the drugs needed further trials to ensure the best outcome which would take time. How much longer? Could he withstand being given all this medication? I was rather concerned for him. The reports regarding his progress were reassuring and the staff were always ready to explain to me what was being done to improve Ian's condition. I was hopeful that he would be able to return nearer to home quite soon.

Chapter 29

Ian was a patient at Billingham Grange for a period of three and a half months returning to the home in York in December 2014. He was heavily sedated for his return journey in an ambulance. I was advised when he was back in his room and I was then able to visit him.

I dreaded what was yet to come. My heart was breaking to see the man I had loved for more than 50 years become somebody I no longer knew. It was agonising and so frustrating. Feeling helpless I went to visit him and was delighted to find there was a glimmer of light. My spirits were lifted and so I felt were Ian's. But how could I be sure? Communication with him was somewhat limited but he was coming out of the months, weeks, and days of what had seemed like a permanent sleep! There had been phases of awareness, but they were short-lived. We had spent a few anxious months watching all this happen hoping to see an improvement, but at times it seemed to be more of a decline.

I walked into his room and he was lying on his bed not moving or opening his eyes. At first, I was distraught. A nurse came into the room and told me Ian was fine and just sleeping off the sedation which had been administered to keep him calm on the journey from Stockton on Tees. She emphasized that it was carefully controlled and not doing any harm to him.

After what seemed a long time he began to stir and looked straight at me. A smile came over his face. It was incredible and made me feel so happy. I was astounded that he seemed to recognise me, and I felt elated. Maybe I could communicate with him now. He seemed to understand what I said. I told him I loved him and to my amazement he responded. At first it was a quiet grunt, but he told me he loved me too. A tear fell

Ready for our Golden Anniversary

onto my cheek. A glimmer of hope. There was light at the end of the tunnel, but we must take each day as it comes. Perhaps it would now be worth organising a bit of a celebration for our forthcoming Golden Wedding Anniversary. Would it be overwhelming for Ian to be surrounded by too many people. or would it have the opposite affect having all his family around him? I would have to give it some thought.

We went ahead with a small celebration. Ruth was the hostess in her usual wonderful way and made a day of heartache into a day of wonderment. Golden celebration balloons festooned the table, and everyone arrived to wait for the man himself! I went to the home to collect Ian. He had no concept of where he was going and why. Who was I doing this for? Was it helping him or was it just for me? That was not the intention. It was for both of us as well as our family to enjoy being together. My heart ached in the longing that Ian would enjoy the celebration of our 50 years as man and wife. A great achievement. What 50 years I asked myself? I could recollect but what about Ian? He does not remember any of it now. He does not know who I am nor the rest of his loving family. What was all this about that he cannot recall any of his life. Not only his life with me, but his childhood and teenage years, all gone! It is so bewildering and rather sad.

"By the time someone with Alzheimer's Disease has forgotten who their family members are, they have lost all sense of who they are, who they were, where they have been, or where they are going. Alzheimer's is not just a disease of forgetting things, friends, or family. Alzheimer's kills an individual slowly, with no compassion and lots of cruelty. By the time a body gives out and fails to function as a living being, the mind, spirit and soul have long been gone.

The slow path towards death is cruel. It rips away at a person's book of life with sharp paper cuts, one page at a time."

They say Alzheimer's patients return to their childhood. I saw no evidence of this with Ian other than him wanting to go and find his Mum. I had tried many times to help him recognise family showing him photographs of his sisters and parents. He had no idea who they were. There was a photograph of him aged 8 or 9 on the door of his room at the nursing home for recognition so he would know it was his room, but he did not know it was him.

I felt incredibly sad for him, but he was not aware. All his life wiped from the slate. Wiped from his mind! The love we shared, obliterated. The love of his parents and siblings, not to mention his very own children and grandchildren, all gone. I saw my husband, but he did not see me. Who did he see? He did see me but who am I? A smile came across his face. "Hello chick" he said. My heart leapt. He seemed to know me today! What is going on in his head? Can someone tell me and why am I not able to have back the man I love? Questions that have no real answers! Sad though the true facts are he has gone forever. I long to have him home and hold him close.

To tell him I love him and want to look after him, in sickness and in health. He would not cope at home now and I would be unable to cope too despite sometimes thinking I could. I had to remind myself of times past and the difficulties we had. Looking back there were scenarios that could have been happening because the illness was already there. Nobody realised at the time. There had been many occasions of an aggressive nature causing great frustration and upset. Had I known the cause could I have made a difference? Alzheimer's Disease is an unknown quantity. Not enough is known about the cause of the disease only how it progresses and destroys the person.

Chapter 30

Ian was at the stage where his medication was controlling his aggressiveness and psychosis. It was decided he could be moved to a residential nursing home with a dementia unit. It was up to me and our children to find a suitable facility. We were given some guidance from the mental health team and social services and a list of available homes together with a brochure with photographs and details. I needed to visit the homes to assess them for myself and to quantify suitability for Ian. Ruth came along with me to help me and to give her opinion. The second home we went to see was quite shocking. Our initial reaction was to give it the benefit of the doubt but the more we saw, the more we disliked. It had an air of coldness and there was a smell of urine which can often be a problem in such places. The corridors seemed narrow. The décor was drab and uninviting. This was not the place to bring Ian. I was almost in tears as we left at the thought of having to move him there. I rang our contact at social services and told her it was not suitable. We had already visited another home which had been totally different, but we were given the impression this did not come within our choices. It had a very welcome feeling the moment we walked in. It was nicely decorated and gave an air of happiness. There were no nasty smells! However, I was pleasantly surprised and delighted to learn that Ian could have a place at this home. A very satisfactory situation given the circumstances of his illness and the fact that he needed constant nursing care and supervision. It was closer to my home too. I would have much preferred to be bringing him home with me though.

A date was set for Ian's move and he was eventually transferred to his new residence by ambulance. I was advised not to visit him for a few days to give him time to settle into his new surroundings.

Chapter 31

Life for Ian in the home proved to be good. He seemed to be quite settled and enjoyed the daily activities which were varied and entertaining. He had a good rapport with the staff and had made them laugh on several occasions. They all loved him and said what a gentleman he was. He had taken a liking to spending time in the nurses' office which was easily accessible from the corridor where he walked backwards and forwards throughout the day. He would help himself to a couple of the fruit pastilles sitting on the desk as he passed by much to the amusement of the nurses who had encouraged him to have a sweet. On my visits it was quite a normal routine for Ian to be wandering around and I regularly had to wander round myself until I found him, asking staff if they had seen him. Several times when I eventually found Ian he would be in another patient's room and refused to move just sitting there quite comfortably. No wonder it took me a while sometimes to locate him. He was quite happy and not willing to move. I had no other option but to sit there with him for the time being until he decided in his own time that he was moving on.

The daily activities included regular entertainment for patients and visitors with a variety of singers who would come along to the home for a couple of hours in an afternoon. The home produced a weekly programme of events so that patients and visitors were aware what was organised. It was good to see them enjoying themselves and joining in with some of the songs. Sometimes even dancing along to the music. There were artistic activities too and everyone was able to take part if they wished. All the events were very well organised and a great benefit to the patients. I was always happy to be there with Ian to enjoy the singing and activities. I would occasionally stay with him to have lunch or tea which the home was always ready to provide if required. It meant I could be there with Ian a bit longer. Chatting to other relatives was very meaningful. We were always sympathetic to one another and discussed situations regarding the progression of the disease and how it affected the patients. It helped to know we were there for one another in a time of need. The staff were always available too and ready to give advice if, and when it was required.

Sometimes Ian would remain in his room not doing anything much at all. He did not watch the TV I had taken in for him. This was something he had stopped doing some time ago, but I hoped he might start watching it now that he was more settled and in a happier environment. I occasionally tried to get him interested if there was some snooker on or rugby which I knew he used to enjoy. However, despite my positive attitude in helping him to watch a programme and talk him through what was on the screen he did not show any sign of interest at all. I realised he probably did not have the ability to concentrate due to his cognitive impairment. This was quite upsetting. It was as though the TV was not there. He had always been a snooker fan and would look forward to watching the matches. I did my best to encourage him to take an interest in the games trying to talk to him about the players and the scores. He just continued staring into space. It was of no interest to him.

One afternoon on my visit, I was amused when Ian decided to twist and turn the knob on his wardrobe door making it screech loudly. It was certainly keeping him entertained and he continued twisting the knob backwards and forwards as it squeaked and squeaked. After a while of putting up with the noise I could stand it no longer and asked him why he was doing it. He said he did not know but continued a while longer until I asked him again to please stop making that awful noise. By then he seemed to have had enough himself and sat down in his chair. I made a mental note to bring some oil with me on my next visit.

Occasionally the box of old photographs I had put together made a welcome pastime, looking through them to try to help Ian recall his family and himself as a child. Each time I went through the process I was hopeful that Ian would begin to recognise something amongst the photographs but despite trying my best it would always become an upsetting scenario when I realised this was not going to happen. I just hoped something would ignite a spark, but he had lost all recollection of his life. I would not let myself feel remorseful although at the back of my mind I felt what had been the point to our lives. I quickly brushed these thoughts aside with the overwhelming feeling of immense pride for our long life together and the reality that it did happen and was incredible at the time. We were very much in love throughout our lives together. I would do it all again, but without this awful unpredictable course our lives have taken. We should be enjoying our retirement together as we had planned. I had to keep focussed on the here and now.

I sometimes wondered what was happening in Ian's head and this was particularly so one day when we were in his room in the home. We were sitting quietly, and I was playing shadows music on my phone which Ian had

always enjoyed. He stood up and walked over to the chest of drawers pointing to the edge of it. He was saying something to me, which was unusual for him to do these days, particularly unprompted. I was finding it finding it difficult to understand what he said and was anxious to hear him before the moment passed and was gone from his mind.

He was mumbling the same word again. As I got close to him the word was plain enough but not a word I had ever heard of "Esalexalox". Maybe it was some form of medication. Nothing was obvious on the chest of drawers other than a shadow. What on earth did he see? What was he trying to tell me? This was so frustrating. If only I could understand. I gave him a kiss and got hold of his hand to sit him down again and as I did so he made a clicking sound with his tongue and chuckled. It was so funny but confusing. I was concerned that I might be missing something he was trying to tell me, but he seemed happy enough.

Most of my days were now taken up with visiting Ian although there were many occasions when I honestly felt it was futile. Ian seemed to be totally unaware that I was there.

Items would go missing from his room. His glasses were often somewhere else. One popular hiding place was behind a curtain in the main sitting room. Clothes would not be in his wardrobe and toiletries would go missing but they often turned up again days later. I learned not to let it bother me until Ian's favourite Aussie hat was no longer found hanging on the back of his bedroom door. I spoke to staff about it who promised to keep their eyes open for it. Ian had bought it in Australia at a local village store whilst on a day trip, visiting areas of the rain forest during our holiday of a lifetime. He loved his Aussie hat and had worn it a lot in the past. However, I realised it probably meant nothing to him now. Sadly, it never did turn up.

Chapter 32

Ian continued to do well at the home. I would sit with him for a few hours but there would be no conversation even though I continued to try and encourage it. I would speak to him telling him what I had been doing and maybe talk to him about our family. There was never any response and I was unsure whether he understood what I was saying but was unable to respond or simply that he just did not hear me.

On a nice day we would go out into the garden and sit for a while in the sunshine. If he needed a shave, I would shave him or maybe cut his nails, although these jobs were usually done by the carers. I was quite happy to take care of him and felt I was making myself useful.

The outside area for patients and staff was comfortable and relaxing and enjoyed by us when we visited too. The garden was well cared for and patients were encouraged to spend time out there on warm, sunny days. Strawberries plants were grown in hanging baskets and everyone took great delight in wandering amongst them picking the fruits to eat and enjoy. It was such a lovely idea.

Ian would occasionally join other patients in the dining room for his meals and I went home leaving him in their company. There were times when he had a meal in his room, and I stayed with him and enjoyed lunch too. As time progressed and the disease worsened Ian was given soft food to enable him to swallow more easily. This is one of the horrendous symptoms as Alzheimer's Disease destroys the brain cells and the messages to parts of the body begin to fail. I was often at the home at mealtimes and the staff were quite happy for me to help Ian eat his food. I had to be vigilant in ensuring each time he had a mouthful that he had swallowed it before I put any more food into his mouth.

There were some worrying moments when I was back home and received a phone call to inform me that Ian had fallen and banged his head. These injuries were usually minor and eventually healed. However, I was sadly aware he was gradually deteriorating. I tried not to dwell on it, but I knew the signs consistent with the disease having learned on the caring and coping course, but it was so hard to accept that it was really happening to Ian. I had seen it with other patients but put it to the back of my mind hoping it would not happen to Ian.

I remember a very poignant demonstration of the progression of Alzheimer's Disease whilst attending the course. The demonstration consisted of three pages of bookshelves. The first page was full of books indicating a normal person. The second page showed the bookshelves with a few missing books – the initial memory loss with the first indication that there is a problem. And on the third page, the bookshelves gradually became emptier showing the deterioration in the brain's ability to function.

It was obvious that this was exactly what was happening to Ian and it was heart breaking. I had to do my utmost to keep him going for as long as possible.

Chapter 33

During the next few months Ian remained much the same. He was still mobile and continued to walk around the home. One of the happy wanderers along with Ian, was Norma. She would suddenly open the door to Ian's room and walk in with a big smile on her face. Quite often she would quickly walk out again. She wore a nice wig which sometimes became dislodged, or she would have it on backwards. I would occasionally adjust it for her when she stood still for long enough. There were occasions when the wig was missing altogether, and poor Norma did not have any hair at all. She never stayed in the room for long but a few minutes later she would appear again. Ian's denture would often be missing, and I was never sure whether it was Ian who had lost it or whether it had been lying around in his room and had been picked up by one of the patients. Ian always managed without it until it turned up again.

It was November 2016, and my birthday was approaching. Birthdays were no longer the same since Ian was totally unaware. Neither did he remember his own birthday or any of his family and friends. I felt sad and upset for him. He no longer had the ability to look forward to the good things in his life. Something we all take for granted. It is so nice to enjoy moments of excitement and happiness at the prospect of an approaching birthday, easter, the festive season, holidays, and many other things that help us to look forward with renewed energy. Family always made my birthdays a special occasion. However, just a couple of days before, I was at home in the early evening when the landline phone rang. It was the home asking for me and I was immediately alert and concerned. Ian had inhaled liquid and had been vomiting. An ambulance had been called and was on the way to hospital with him. I left immediately in my car. On arrival at the accident and emergency department I was eventually taken to the cubicle where Ian was being assessed. The nurse was inserting a needle into Ian's arm to get antibiotics into him as quickly as possible but was struggling to find a vein. Another nurse tried on his other arm, but also had problems. Ian remained calm throughout and eventually they succeeded, and he was left to settle down. He was also given an intravenous drip to rehydrate him. Within a few days he was well enough to go back to the home.

This situation proved to be the pattern to Ian's life over a period of several weeks and into the Christmas period. I would dread the phone ringing in case it was the home with bad news again. Despite being monitored whilst having a meal and only eating soft food, Ian was struggling to swallow properly. Ensuring that he had swallowed before putting more food into his mouth was vital.

I was losing count of Ian's hospital admissions. One of the nurses at the home came to have a chat with me and advised that Ian's body could only go through so much. He was becoming weaker each time he had to be put through the trauma. I was devastated but knew this really was the kindest way forward. There was no alternative the time had come, and sadly I was going to have to let him go.

As my hospital visits increased, I was quite thankful to have the help of one of my friends from carers' café who lived much closer to the hospital and was able to park in a disabled space, saving me having to leave my car for long periods of time costing a large amount in parking fees. Rick would meet me at a convenient location to park my car and then take me to the hospital. It was always nice to have his company too.

He picked me up to take me back to my car when I was ready to go home or would wait in his car in the hospital car park.

Chapter 34

Ian's release from the rigours of this devastating disease was drawing near. I had been sitting by his bedside in hospital for 2 days and 2 nights, going home briefly after the first night to freshen up but I was quite anxious to get back to his bedside and be there for him.

I was told he only had a few hours to live when arriving in Resus after receiving the call from the home. I could hear his very congested breathing as I entered the area where he was being assessed and given medication. I had to let our children know what was happening. Ruth was able to come to the hospital immediately, but Roger and Andrew had had a drink or two continuing the New Year celebrations so were unable to be there straight away. Andrew arrived to stay overnight with me on the second night. Ian was being given morphine and other medication to keep him comfortable, but his heavy noisy breathing was quite distressing.

He was eventually moved to a private room and end of life care was put in place. I felt numb at what I was witnessing. It did not seem real. I should be terribly upset, but I was in a daze. The man I lived with and loved for over 50 years was nearing the end of his life. Our life together. But it would be a relief when he was no longer suffering. Sadly, this was the only way. There was no cure.

I sat by his bedside and gave him some moisture on a cotton bud, holding his hand, moving closer to him watching his every breath. I had just been to the Nurses' station to ask for some help, some relief for the rattling noise he was making. They asked me to leave the room whilst attending to him. I was extremely anxious waiting to go back to Ian. On my return to his bedside, he was extremely pale, but his breathing was much quieter and seemed to be slowing. I gave him a kiss and told him I loved him. Every minute now was precious. Till death us do part echoed in my head and pictures of us standing at the alter feeling happy and looking forward to our future together flashed by me. No! I want my man back, the man I married. We were going to be together forever. I was instantly brought back to my senses as his breathing became irregular. I watched him closely and in one incredible moment he breathed his last. I could not take my eyes off him hoping for another breath, but the love of my life was gone. He was now at peace free from the illness.

I had to find Andrew to tell him. He had gone to find a more comfortable chair to get a bit of sleep. He was immediately on his feet and back by the hospital bed with his Dad for the last time. Although we were both upset, we felt a wave of relief and an intense moment of calmness.

At home in the early hours and in much need of some sleep, I was in my flat, getting ready for bed, when a faint sound reached my ears. A very gentle, warming voice simply said hi. I immediately turned round expecting to see Andrew, but there was no-one there. I certainly heard a voice. The room felt cosy, and a warmth surrounded. I realised the voice I had heard was Ian's. He had come home to me, free from the years under the spell of dementia. I felt a great sense of comfort. He was there with me and will remain with me forever. As it was in life is now in death. Our lifelong memories will linger on.

Chapter 35

We all spent some time saying our goodbyes to Ian as he lay peacefully at the funeral parlour. Ruth had kept a lock of her lovely blonde hair from her first hair cut as a child. She placed it beside her Dad as a sign of her everlasting love, remembering all those wonderful times she spent with him. Roger held a picture which he lovingly laid next to Ian to treasure forever as a reminder of the special love between father and son. It was a picture of the herb valerian which Ian and I had adopted as an emblem of our lives together entwining our names as one. Andrew gave his Dad his love and admiration as he sat with us in the hospital during the final hours of Ian's life. Such memorable treasures passed on to remain forever in all our hearts.

It was a chilly but bright January morning in 2017. I was at home with Ruth, and we were both feeling that the day ahead would be a difficult one. Previously, together with Roger and Andrew, we had spent several hours with the funeral director and the celebrant, organising Ian's funeral. He had never been religious and always said he did not want a fuss, or a lot of money spending on his funeral. In fact, he wanted a simple goodbye. This was exactly what the family organised. A celebration of Ian's life. His achievements, of which there were plenty and stories of his life with his family and friends. The music he loved played a huge part. His lifelong friend, Tony, paid a fitting tribute on the keyboard and everyone began to sing. It was all very heart warming and Ian would have been so pleased with his send off. I made it quite clear I did not want any of us to feel rushed into saying our goodbyes and was told I could organise an additional period to enable everyone to have a chance to say their farewells. My final wish had been to place candles on the coffin as a sign of the love we all felt for Ian.

The events of the day were all very memorable. The wake was held close to the crematorium and was very well attended.

Though such a sad day, it was enjoyed by everyone just as Ian would have wanted.

We all celebrated his life, enjoying good food and drink together and plenty of conversation as the day came to an end.

Several months later, family and friends gathered at Pickering in North Yorkshire to take Ian's ashes on a steam train. An event organised by the North Yorkshire Moors Railway. All his life Ian had loved steam engines and I had been on many outings with him to see them working or to enjoy a day out on a steam train. He enjoyed watching steam at work in its many forms, trains being a favourite in his youth. Everyone had an enjoyable journey to Grosmont. I had talked to the engine driver and fireman, jumping up onto the footplate to have a look where the cask containing Ian's ashes would go as the train worked hard pulling the carriages up an incline. The casket was to be placed in the fire as the train whistle tooted loudly in celebration to inform everyone. Ian could now enjoy being around the steam trains forever and whenever he wished. Our glasses were raised to toast Ian. It had been a gratifying day and a sad goodbye but also one I knew only too well Ian would have loved.

Everyone thoroughly enjoyed a good lunch at the Station Hotel close to Grosmont Station and took the return journey to Pickering a couple of hours later after a very memorable day.

Chapter 36

I continue to think about Ian on most days. Past events will pop into my head from time to time recalling what he had to suffer during his illness and recollections of the good times. I often wonder if the situation regarding his illness could have been handled differently. The kicking of the doors and banging on windows, his aggressiveness with me and our family had happened on several occasions, but it was never related to an illness or memory problems until it progressed. The fact that he was sectioned and then never came home again not long afterwards horrifies me. He had to be detained. Did he understand this? Did he know what was happening to him? As Alzheimer's progressed maybe he tried to communicate his fears but was unable to find the words. The agony of knowing something is wrong but not knowing what it is or how to fix it must be an imprisonment of the mind. To be lost in a world you no longer recognize is a daily struggle. No-one should have to suffer the indignities consistent with Alzheimer's Disease.

Quality of life is bad, but I found it hard to ever consider ending his life. The moment I was advised to agree to end of life care for Ian was a heart stopping moment. I felt sick knowing the end was near. The thought of losing the love of my life made me feel there was no point to my life. But this is not what we discussed. Life goes on for whoever is left in a relationship and life is to be lived.

Chapter 37

Two years after he had gone, I still missed him very much and always will. His laughter, the sound of his voice, his brilliant mind, his company, our long walks together along the beach in Spain. But somehow, I always felt that he was somewhere nearby sometimes doing his own thing. Travelling on and sharing a kind of blessing with me, just as he had when he was alive before dementia took over his mind and body. Knowing and loving him has been my greatest gift.

The advances of Research into possible causes of Dementia

2019/2020: In the light of current reports regarding head trauma relating to the cause of dementia and several ex-footballers being diagnosed with this awful disease, apparently caused by heading the ball, I now wonder if maybe Ian had suffered a head trauma when he was struck by the catapult stone in his youth. We will never know the answer to this although of course, the scan of his brain did not pick up a problem.

Our candle of love is burning.
On this your special day.
To hold you again I am yearning,
To bring you home to stay.
But you are at peace now, resting at last.
The dementia that took you all gone.
I have my love back as he was in the past.
To hold onto forever since we two became one.
Our candle flame will never die,
Just like the love between you and I.
You will always hold a special place in my heart.
One that said we were never to part.
Until the day we are together again.
We will share precious moments now, and then.

You are always with me.

My Greatest Gift

Valerian

Our names entwined forever in the herb valerian

Acknowledgements

The Alzheimer's Society, York.
Psychiatric Consultants, Nurses and Carers, York NHS Trust.
Local Mental Health Team and Carers.
Billingham Grange, Billingham, Stockton on Tees.
St. Catherine's Residential & Nursing Home, Shipton by
Beningbrough, York.
Carer's Café, The Bothy, Deans Garden Centre, Stockton on
the Forest, York.

*Thank you to you all for caring for Ian
and for helping me.*

Printed in Great Britain
by Amazon

61685360R00066